ILY WAMH...
4-EVER
I.W.

12-16-82

ILY WAMH...
4-EVER
I.W.

Play Better
Tennis
with
Billie Jean King
and Reginald Brace

Play Better Tennis

with
Billie Jean King
and Reginald Brace

octopus

Contents

First published 1981 by
Octopus Books Limited
59 Grosvenor Street
London W1

Printed in Hong Kong

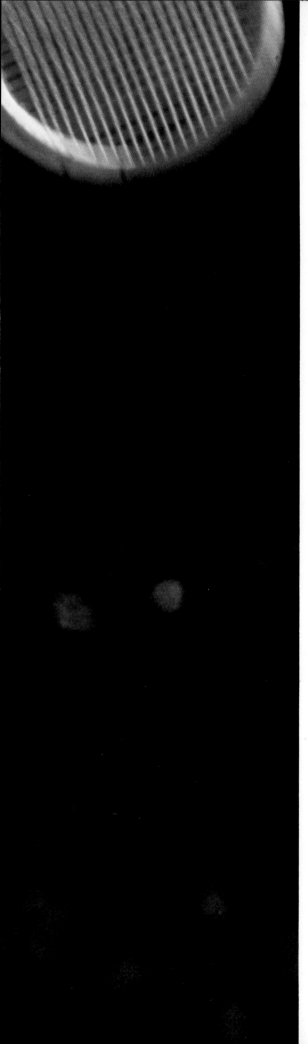

Preface

As Billie Jean King says within these pages, tennis instruction books are a dime-a-dozen these days. So why did we produce this one? Simply in the belief that Billie Jean's vast experience will give readers a fresh insight into the game and a renewed appetite for playing it.

Although the basics are included, the book is directed at players who do not need to be introduced to the rudiments of tennis but are anxious to improve the standard of their performance. Billie Jean feels that tennis is as much about attitude as aptitude and this is the theme we have tried to develop.

Speaking as a club player of limited ability but boundless optimism I can vouch for the value of Billie Jean's shrewd advice. It is a book for men and women and there is a strong emphasis on doubles, the game that most tennis people play.

The book is the outcome of long conversations in London, Brighton and Paris and I am grateful to John Edwards, Editor of the Yorkshire Post, for his benevolent attitude towards my involvement in its preparation. Billie Jean and myself hope that it will justify its title and point the way towards playing better tennis.

Reginald Brace, September, 1980.

Impressions of Billie Jean King

Quotations from the players record their undisguised admiration for the matchless contribution Billie Jean King has made to the game of tennis.

Arthur Ashe:
'The Seventies were a time of phenomenal growth for tennis and Billie Jean King was one of the prime movers behind that growth. I nominate Billie Jean without reservation, as my Player of the Seventies. Besides her remarkable talent she brought to tennis a spirit and a personality that took the game from a highbrow pastime to almost a national mania. She accomplished this with rare outspokenness, dedication and generosity. Where some other contemporary stars have simply taken home their winnings Billie Jean has given something special back to the game.'

Chris Lloyd:
'I admire Billie Jean for the battles she fought for women's tennis. She helped to pave the way for me and other women tennis players. I also admire her personally for her guts and determination on the tennis court. She has an incomparable passion for the game.'

Tracy Austin:
'I have always thought of Billie Jean as a great leader, on and off the court. She has proved this to be true in a long and distinguished career.'

Jimmy Connors:
'Billie Jean pretty well started women's tennis in the sense of the professional game. She has also been an influential figure in getting people who knew little about tennis interested in the game. I'm talking about her match against Bobby Riggs, which had enormous TV and Press coverage, and also her belief in World Team Tennis which took tennis to the public. I always enjoyed playing Team Tennis and I'm sure Billie Jean did. I wouldn't mind at all if it came back in a couple of years' time. In fact, I'd welcome a chance to play Team Tennis again when my tournament career is over. As a player, well, there is no stronger competitor than Billie Jean. Every time she goes out and plays a match, she is eager and fights to the death. She's got a wonderful attitude, which accounts for all the championships she has won.'

On court

Psychology • Team tennis • Winning
Weaknesses • Strengths • Planning
Highs • Lows

What tennis means to me

Billie Jean discusses the reasons why she keeps on playing—the creativity involved in the game, the pleasure she derives from it and the pursuit of perfection which made her into a champion.

When I celebrated my birthday at a tournament in Brighton, England, last November, the K-shaped cake had 21 flickering candles on it. But the lungs that blew the candles out were 36 years old. I made no secret of the fact. I was born on November 22, 1943 and I have been playing tennis since I was 10. Although I am not quite ready for the rocking chair and I *hate* being called the Old Lady of the circuit, I have been around a long time by the standards of a professional game where teenagers get tougher every year.

The game has always meant a lot to me from the day I first clutched a racket and decided that I wanted to be the best player in the world. It still does and I know it always will. But the reason for writing this book is not to populate the world's tennis courts with Billie Jean Kings; it is an honest attempt to transfer my enthusiasm for tennis to you, the reader, to help you to enjoy your own game more and make you a better player in the process.

It would not be stretching it too far to say that my affection for tennis amounts to a love affair. My husband Larry would probably describe it as a marriage! Like most relationships, it has had its fair share of low moments—including three major knee operations and foot surgery—which have sunk my spirits to the level of a drop shot. But I've always come back after getting rid of the crutches and each time has provided a fresh kick, despite the exercises and the ice packs I need to keep my particular show on the road.

Why do I keep on playing?

People never stop asking me why I carry on playing. My answer is, does a painter stop painting when he reaches a certain age, or a musician stop playing? I love tennis. Just because you are a professional does not mean that you can't have a warmth towards the sport that you play. I could not live the life I lead without genuinely loving the game, which I regard as an art, a science and a continuing challenge.

It is certainly not the glamour of the life which keeps me going. Believe me, there is not much glamour in the rituals I have to observe to keep myself in shape. It might look glamorous on court. That's your time on stage. You are performing, and you enjoy it—particularly if you are playing well, and winning! But when you leave the ground or the stadium you only have time for dinner, your washing, and getting yourself together for your next match. That's not glamour.

A form of self-expression

I think the simplest explanation of why tennis has dominated a huge slice of my life is the extreme pleasure I get from playing it. This might not always be apparent on court when I'm locked in a private world of concentration or muttering to myself in stage whispers which can be heard at the other end of the arena. But tennis is the ultimate form of self-expression for me. The joy it brings is something money cannot buy. You have to create that satisfaction yourself, and the only way to create

In a consumer-orientated world it is nice to be able to produce something for yourself. This is why I derive such tremendous satisfaction from just hitting a tennis ball and producing a shot. There is no shop in the world where you can buy a backhand down the line—but you can make your own. Tennis gives you a chance to be creative as well as competitive, to be a producer as opposed to a mere consumer, to do it yourself instead of having it done for you.

it is by hard and constructive effort whether you are a top pro or a weekend club player.

I still get a thrill just from hitting a tennis ball and I believe this is because I have had to learn to produce the shot myself. Most people in the world are consumers—very few are producers. How many people do you know who work simply for a pay cheque without doing anything remotely creative for most of their lives? Well, tennis gives you a chance to produce something for yourself. There is no shop in the world where you can buy a great backhand down the line, but you can make your own—and I hope this book will help you to do it.

Tennis is good for you

In a way, tennis for me is like Margot Fonteyn and ballet. She still works out to keep her body in shape. It is part of her being, an integral part of living. I am not suggesting that the non-professional player should be as goal-orientated as me, but I believe that tennis is good for you physically, mentally and socially. Most of us are naturally gregarious and tennis is a wonderful way of meeting people, not just beating them. It can teach you to think quickly under stress, and there is nothing to equal that feeling of relaxation after a long, tough match.

Tennis is not an easy game to play. A great game, yes, but a hard one to learn—in fact, you never really stop learning. They say that golf is difficult but at least a golf ball is motionless when you try to hit it. There are so many variables in tennis, and of course this is one of the fascinations of the game. The ball never comes across the same twice in your whole lifetime, which I think is fantastic.

You can practise as long as you like but you can never rehearse a game of tennis. When you walk on court there is nothing predictable about any rally. In musical terms it is more like the improvisations of a rock or jazz musician than a piece by Tchaikovsky where all the notes are written down. Tennis is all about spontaneity and reacting to unexpected situations as they arise. This is what makes it so intriguing, and worth mastering despite the perseverance that mastery usually involves.

When things go wrong

There are times when, no matter how proficient you are, it does not seem worth the struggle. I know that feeling when you want to bag it, call it a day and take up something less demanding. I have hurled my rackets into a corner in disgust, but as they were flying across the room I've been saying, 'Come back, come back. Without you I would never have been able to travel,

The continuing challenge of tennis fascinates me. No matter how hard you practice, you can never rehearse what happens out there on court. The tennis court is a place for spontaneity and improvisation as you react to the unexpected in the ebb and flow of a match. Tennis is the ultimate form of self-expression for me, although the pleasure I get from playing might not always be apparent when I'm locked in a private world of concentration trying to work out how to get the ball over the net more often than my opponent.

never been able to excel at something, never been able to experience those fleeting moments of joy which only tennis can bring.'

When I was a school kid back home in Long Beach the teacher used to give us 20 minutes when we could do anything we wanted. I was the only child in the classroom to look at the map. I would stare at countries like England, France and Japan and say, 'One day I'm going to go to all those places'. I didn't know how, because my parents certainly couldn't afford to send me. But something inside me always insisted that I would get there, and I did. Tennis was my passport, and that's why I never could throw my rackets in the drink. Or if I did, I would always drag them right out again.

Aiming for perfection
For many years now I have had this tag of being a natural competitor. This is how the media describe me, and how the public see me. But it is not quite true. Of course I am competitive, but perfection is my number one goal in tennis. In other words, I am more of a perfectionist than a competitor. When you see me bellowing at myself on court, it's not necessarily because I've just lost a point. I've probably done a less than perfect shot. My main battles out there are against myself.

This might seem a curious admission after 25 years of tournament competition which have brought 20 Wimbledon titles, and 30 US Women's titles, not to mention the championships of France, Australia and Italy. But I am not competitive in the way that some players are. I don't sit and play games like the others do. They play electronic games or cards and they really want to beat the kid on the other side of the table. Those pursuits are of no interest to me at all. Of course I compete at tennis— but first and foremost I am a perfectionist trying to play the game as well as it can be played. The media's impression of me is one-dimensional and so, inevitably, is that of the public.

My retirement from singles
Another illusion that many people have about me is that I've retired from singles more times than Frank Sinatra has retired from singing. Actually I only said it once, and that was in 1975 after I had won the Wimbledon singles for the sixth time. I was in fantastic condition when I left Wimbledon but by January the following year I was positively rotund, waddling around and completely out of shape. I wasted 1976. After watching Chris Evert and Evonne Cawley play the final at Wimbledon I asked myself what I was doing. I realized how

much healthier and happier I had felt playing singles as well as doubles. So, despite my age and the operations, the Old Lady came back and I haven't regretted it.

Although there was a gap in my life when I was not playing in tournaments so much, I am the kind of person who can fill the gaps. Tennis is important but I'm happy doing a lot of things. I don't think that when I eventually give up serious competition I will feel the same sort of emptiness some players do when it is time to call it a day. I have a lot of interests. Retirement will not be a void or an abyss, merely a chance to do other things.

My competitive career will end on the day when tournament play is no longer fun for me, when I can't handle losing as much, or it hurts too much physically, or I want to spend more time with Larry. Injury is the great problem. It bothers me when I am unable to give 100 per cent, and injury

I never really liked the United States championships when they were held at Forest Hills. Maybe it had something to do with my first experience of the place as a teenager in 1959. Karen Hantze had whetted my anticipation but I remember being disappointed by the West Side Tennis Club, the state of the grass courts, the condition of the dressing rooms and the pomposity of some of the officials. In the first match I played there I was beaten after holding match point. But it was still a matter of great pride to win the US title there in 1967 (beating Ann Haydon Jones in the final), 1971 (Rosie Casals), 1972 (Kerry Melville) and 1974 (Evonne Goolagong).

means just that. When you're injured you lose a lot more matches, and after a time it affects you emotionally. There comes a stage when it hardly seems worth it for you, or for the people around you.

A game for a lifetime
They say you're as old as you feel, and it's true. Some people are as old at 26 as I feel at 36. But, although it has become something of a cliché, tennis really is a game for a lifetime. I remember a US tennis official telling me when I was 12, 'Billie, you're playing a game for a lifetime', and I recall thinking, 'Lifetime—heck, I just want to play at Wimbledon'. But here I am in my mid-thirties, and the statement has become more meaningful to me.

Every age you go through has its pluses and minuses. One of the minuses of being my age is that you know you can't keep going out there and performing indefinitely. I think that Nureyev has similar feelings, which is why he is dancing with such a sense of urgency. That is the reason I have tried to crowd as much tennis as possible into the past year. Each moment is precious and I lead a full tennis life because I know it will not last forever.

One plus for me is that at least I know the value of what I have in the same way that Ken Rosewall does. Neither of us is young—Ken is even older than I am!—but the tennis we play is drawn from a lifetime's experience. Your game can mature as you grow older, you can learn to appreciate it more, and there is always some aspect of it that you can improve or work on.

Getting things into perspective
One thing tennis has taught me in the years since I was Billie Jean Moffitt, the Californian chatterbox, is the ability to laugh at myself—by that I mean it's given me a sense of perspective. If I lose I might act as though it is the end of the world but the sun rises the next day whether you have won or lost so you might as well bounce right back and greet it. It might seem a big deal while you are out there busting your gut and going crazy, but you must be able to look back and smile.

Being American has helped me in a way. If I were from a small European country and had done what I have done in tennis, I would have it made. In the United States there is no resting on laurels. They just look at me and say, 'OK, Billie, but what are you

When I was 12, a US tennis official said to me 'Billie, you are playing a game for a lifetime.' I remember thinking 'Lifetime, heck—I just want to play at Wimbledon.' I used to dream about the place. Three years before I even went there I wrote a school English essay about Wimbledon which went into enormous detail about the event and my progress there! Those were the starry-eyed days and of course your outlook and opinions mature as you grow older. Wimbledon nevertheless remains something special. It is a celebration of the game as much as a championship—an annual gathering of tennis players, lovers of the game and those who merely come to flirt. It is also tradition, a self-perpetuating slice of sporting history. There is nothing to equal the exultation of winning there, and sharing your joy with the Centre Court.

doing *now*?'. It is just a difference in attitude and upbringing. It is today that matters in the USA, not yesterday. Win or lose, it does not do to take yourself too seriously. You have to laugh at your own failings, and that is one of the most helpful things that tennis can teach you.

My best moment

The highest point of my career? This is a question I am asked repeatedly and I tend to come up with a different answer each time. Just for this book I have really tried to arrive at something definite, and I have to say that winning the Wimbledon doubles with Karen Susman in 1961 was something special to me—my tennis Everest if you like.

She was Karen Hantze then and I was Little Miss Moffitt, all-talking daughter of a Long Beach fire officer. It was my first year at Wimbledon and I beat Margaret Court (she was Smith then) in my opening match which was quite a debut and an imperishable memory in itself.

But, unlike a lot of today's players, doubles has always meant just as much to me as singles, and winning the doubles with Karen was unforgettable. She was fun. I liked her, and still do. We giggled, had a good time and beat Margaret and Jan Lehane 6–3 6–4 in the final. We were the youngest team ever to win the title, and looking back I just cannot top the feeling I had that day.

My 1979 record

It was a totally different sensation on the centre court at the All England Club in 1979 when I nudged my way into Wimbledon history by winning a record twentieth title. It was the women's doubles again, my partner was Martina Navratilova, and we beat Betty Stove and Wendy Turnbull 5–7 6–3 6–2. This enabled me to break Elizabeth Ryan's record of 19 titles but I cannot say it filled me with elation.

Elizabeth collapsed and died at Wimbledon the eve of the final and of course her passing threw something of a shadow over the match. It was a shame, although there is no doubt in my mind that she just didn't want to be alive to see her record broken. She was 88, she had held it for a long, long time and she wanted it for herself. But records are there to be broken. I mean, I haven't finished yet. I want to win 21 Wimbledon titles, or more. I also realize that some day someone will come along and claim my little niche in Wimbledon's hall of fame.

And the worst times

Lows? I think that 1971 and 1972 were the lowest time in my life. Everybody was saying that women's tennis would not get off the ground, I was determined that it would and I overworked. I almost killed myself. I aged a lot in those two years.

I became tired to the point of exhaustion of taking the feedback from cynics and critics who felt that women's tennis couldn't make it on its own. It taught me a lot about human nature, and how some people resist change and will not ever take a chance. The women's tour is now a fact of tennis life and a very successful one, but I will never forget the toll of those early years.

That is one of the reasons why I get a little annoyed with the Press when they keep on asking me, 'When are you going to quit?' It's like the Chinese water torture. Then some players have been known to say, 'There is no way I will be on the circuit at Billie's age.' For heaven's sake, I was 28 when women's tennis began to grow into what it has become today. I have been playing full-time tennis with the opportunities that everybody considers normal today for only eight years. I had none of the scope enjoyed by Tracy Austin or Chris Evert-Lloyd in their teenage years. Money is not everything. In fact, it is a secondary consideration. But I feel that I owe it to myself to enjoy the game now that women's tennis has really come of age.

World Team Tennis

And then, of course, there was the end of World Team Tennis. This was a dream of mine, and Larry's, and people like Dennis Murphy. For me it was all about taking tennis to people who did not go to tournaments or country clubs but wanted to support a team and become part of tennis that way. I felt that was where the future was, and it was heartbreaking when it all ended.

What a first night we had in Philadelphia in 1974: bands, ballyhoo, showmanship and 10,000 spectators. I thought it was the dawn of a new tennis era, and Elton John wrote a song about my team—Philadelphia Freedoms. I said at the time that it might take five years for the idea of inter-city competition to become established, but in the end the dream didn't come true and Team Tennis died in 1978.

I still think it was the only way that tennis was going to be big as a spectator sport. Somebody worked out that in the last year of Team Tennis it was seen by one-quarter of the people who watched any kind of professional tennis. We had something that could have been a huge base for the game with community importance: an inter-relationship with the masses which is enjoyed by teams in other sports, but not in tennis.

This is me on home ground, in the United States. Being American has helped me to keep things in perspective. If I had been born in some small European country and achieved what I have achieved in tennis, I would have it made. But in the United States there is no resting on laurels. It is a case of 'OK, Billie, but what are you doing *now*?' It is today that matters in America not yesterday. Win or lose, you bounce back and move on, and learn not to take yourself too seriously. The ability to laugh at your own failings is one of the most helpful things that tennis can teach you. And, incidentally, just because you are a professional does not mean that you cannot feel a warmth towards the game you play. Apart from being a source of income, tennis for me is an art, a science and, above all, a source of pleasure. Tennis can be enjoyed at any level.

Tennis and the spectators

As players, we give entertainment in tournaments—our souls and all that—for a week, but we rarely get involved with the community concerned. We drift into town, play our tennis, and drift out again. Tennis is always going to remain relatively small in terms of spectators now. I have put Team Tennis behind me in a way, and yet in my heart of hearts I hope that some day we will have it all together again.

Tennis in the United States has slipped from the popularity it enjoyed during its boom years in the mid-1970s. Sales of rackets have fallen and a lot of people who found tennis hard to conquer have moved on to jogging or racket ball—a simpler game involving a bigger racket and a slower ball. I am not too depressed about this; I think the situation is now more realistic because we know what the market really is instead of having an artificial picture of it.

We are still subsidized by sponsorship rather than straight gate receipts, but fortunately, despite the decline, tennis is not short of interested companies who want to be associated with the game. And as tennis in America finds a more sensible level, interest is soaring in Europe and Japan.

There is no need for despondency. I just have that sneaking regret about the death of Team Tennis, for which I fought so hard.

The future of tennis

As far as the future of tennis is concerned—have no fear. It remains a great game, the finest one-to-one confrontation in sport, and it will always hook people attracted by its variety and the stimulus it gives to body and mind.

You can enjoy tennis at any level of the game, whether you are a star competing for money or an average player battling for nothing more than fulfilment and fitness. It's all relative to the people involved; they experience the same anguish, frustration and delight no matter what the environment might be.

It is often said that players should play against somebody of roughly the same standard or a little bit better than themselves. I understand the motive for this, but I have certain reservations. You can have fun playing anybody, and tennis should be fun.

I have played against a 10-year-old who had hardly ever hit a ball and what we did was use half the service box. We cut the area down to make it interesting and we

Martina Navratilova (right) with whom I won the Wimbledon women's doubles in 1979 to set up a personal record of 20 Wimbledon titles. It looks as though I am trying to help the umpire in the picture of myself but the gesture could also be an attempt to indicate the breadth of Martina's huge talent for the game. She owns one of the most feared serves in women's tennis, hits a mean volley and has an athlete's fitness.

On the way to my twentieth Wimbledon title with Martina Navratilova in the final of the women's doubles in 1979. We beat Betty Stove and Wendy Turnbull 5–7 6–3 6–2. The tension shows in both our faces. Curiously, Martina felt it more than me, she was so anxious for me to win that twentieth title.

enjoyed ourselves. Take a three-year-old on court and you can forget the lines and the net. Contact with the ball represents success. You have just got to be flexible and relate to whatever situation you are in.

Starting to play

You certainly don't want someone your own level when you are starting in the game. You want someone a lot better who can feed the ball to you for long periods of time. The first summer I played tournaments I must have lost every match love and love. I was a piece of cake for everybody. You could say that was disastrous and discouraging. I found it exasperating, but beneficial. All those heavy defeats created a challenge which I was determined to meet, and I did.

Always aim for improvement, and try to play about three times a week. Most people play once a week and by doing that they remain static. They are maintaining their game but not enhancing it. By the time their hour is up they are just getting going and then it's all over for another week. Three sessions a week is a big investment in time and money but it's the best way to improve your game.

Planning a game

One of the great delights of life for me remains the planning and execution of a tennis shot—hitting a topspin forehand that will loop into the corner of the court, or moving into the net on a sliced backhand that I know is going to set up a chance for the volley I just love to hit. The feeling is incomparable.

Actually, I am always walking a tightrope on court. My creative half wants to take risks by using variations in spin, direction and pace but the winner in me insists on playing shots with a greater percentage of success. I am invariably on the edge of the ledge and sometimes I have to be more boring than I would like to be just to win. But not totally boring. That streak of self-expression is always breaking through, and when it does winning a point comes second to the pleasure of hitting a difficult shot.

You will have gathered by now that I am a tennis junkie. When I stop playing competitively I would like to coach. One dream of mine is to go around different countries helping top juniors. I think I am a good motivator and I think I can get the most out of players if they have the gift and the desire for tennis.

This book is an attempt to transmit my enjoyment and enthusiasm. I have tried to explain what tennis means to me and what it could mean to you. At the end of the book I hope you will want to play more and play better.

The power of positive tennis

Tennis is a game of the mind and a positive approach often holds the key to success. Billie Jean explains how pressing the right mental buttons can hit the tennis jackpot. You can learn a lot about yourself as you explore the subtleties of tennis.

Tennis instruction books tend to be a dime-a-dozen these days and this book is not intended for the absolute beginner. In getting it together I am assuming that I am talking to people who know one end of a racket from the other and can play the game a bit; people who do not have to be lectured at length about the virtues of keeping the eye on the ball, lively footwork, good balance, controlling the racket swing and rigid concentration. Reminded, perhaps, but not told as if they were recently discovered facets of an ancient game.

Those are fundamentals which anyone who is a player will already know. You will also know that tennis is not a game for stereotypes, automatons or robots. You might try to learn tennis by numbers, as it were, but you cannot play it like that. So much of tennis demands improvisation and split-second thinking that every player evolves his or her own style. It is a sport for individuals and few games expose personal characteristics so vividly.

Mental attitudes
You can be the most benign and benevolent character imaginable off court, but thrust into a stress-filled situation on it you can become John McEnroe and Billie Jean King rolled into one explosive package. Your inner self is exposed for all to see as the tennis court becomes the equivalent of a psychiatrist's couch. I have often thought that a shrewd selling line for the game would be, 'Discover tennis, and find yourself'. Perhaps you do not always like what

you find out, but it is nice to know. Tennis is a character builder which can help you in everyday life.

Let us consider the mental attitudes involved in tennis. There are two types of error in the game, mental and execution. A mental mistake is when your choice of shot is incorrect, and a mistake in execution is when, despite making the right stroke decision, you fail to hit the shot properly. A lot of people miss the difference between the two, but there is a difference and it is an important one.

That is why you will sometimes see a top player seething with anger despite making a winning shot. You might think, 'What's the problem? The point is won.' But the player knows that he made a dumb shot and he was lucky to win the rally. It was a mental error, even if he did get away with it that time.

Thinking tennis
What I am saying is that it is vital to be thinking all the time; not merely producing a shot, but making sure that it is the right shot. If your mental approach is alert and your execution is correct, then you are in business. That is what you must be aiming for all the time and, although it will not happen overnight, it is worth striving for. Thought plus technique equals good tennis.

So much of success in tennis springs from the mind. You can be the greatest physical specimen who ever struck a tennis ball but if there is nothing going on be-

Play for the moment and try not to let your mind brood on something that has already happened, or might happen in a match. Isolate each point from the next and you are taking a positive step towards success through mental discipline.

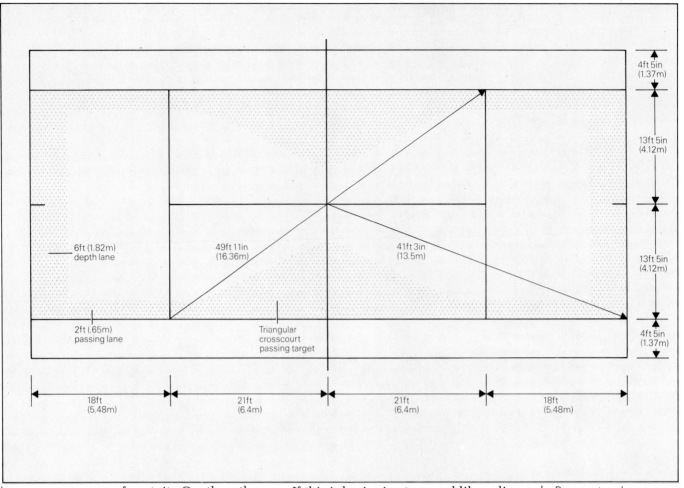

4ft 5in
(1.37m)

13ft 5in
(4.12m)

13ft 5in
(4.12m)

4ft 5in
(1.37m)

6ft (1.82m)
depth lane

49ft 11in
(16.36m)

41ft 3in
(13.5m)

2ft (.65m)
passing lane

Triangular
crosscourt
passing target

18ft
(5.48m)

21ft
(6.4m)

21ft
(6.4m)

18ft
(5.48m)

tween your ears, forget it. On the other hand, you can still be a champion if you are no great shape physically, but are mentally strong. The sharp-witted Davids of tennis can often bring down the non-thinking Goliaths.

A positive approach

Smart tennis players perform within themselves, and know what they can do. They do not brood about their limitations but think in terms of their capacity. It is a positive attitude—like describing a vase as half-full, not half-empty—and that sort of optimistic outlook is of enormous value on a tennis court. I know this is true because it is an outlook I have tried to foster in myself throughout my career.

For example, you are a service break down in the deciding set of an important match. Disaster or challenge? The choice is yours. I always strive to treat critical moments like that as an opportunity to flex my mental muscles, raise my game and hit back. Try not to droop when things are going against you. So you struggle, and you lose—that's too bad. At least you have given the match your best, and you can walk off with your head up. Develop that sort of attitude and you will be pleasantly surprised how it becomes ingrained into your character both in and out of tennis.

If this is beginning to sound like a dissertation on positive thinking, that is not surprising. I am a firm believer in the power of positive thought. Press the right mental buttons and you will be amazed at how often you can hit the tennis jackpot. Think negatively and you can be back in the club house, under the shower, before you know what hit you!

Psycho-Cybernetics

Psycho-Cybernetics may be an unfamiliar term to many people. It is an approach to life and living devised by Dr Maxwell Maltz, one of the world's leading plastic surgeons, and I carry his book on the subject wherever I go. Briefly, it is a way of improving your self-image, or your mental picture of yourself. Usually you act like the person you think you are—that is, if you believe you are a failure you will find some way to fail even if things are going your way. Similarly, if you are convinced that you are a victim of injustice you will instinctively find circumstances to justify your opinion.

Without wishing to over-simplify Dr Maltz's stimulating theories, Psycho-Cybernetics teaches you how to change a pessimistic self-image by discovering the success mechanism within you. This involves breaking old mental habits by taking

Because top players command more power and accuracy they hit with greater depth and closer to the lines. The shaded area in this diagram shows where they direct their shots. The 6 ft (1.82 m) deep alley at the back of the court is the place where their ground strokes and lobs are intended to land. The down the line passing shot is directed at a 2 ft (.6 m) wide lane on either side of the court. The triangular shaded area is the target for crosscourt passing shots. The hourglass shaped zone in the middle is, however, where the ball tends to land most often—even for leading players!

Trajectories
This diagram (right) shows the height achieved by topspin as used by Borg and the lower trajectory of a flatter shot. While the ball soars Borg uses his quickness of foot and eye to get into position for the next shot.

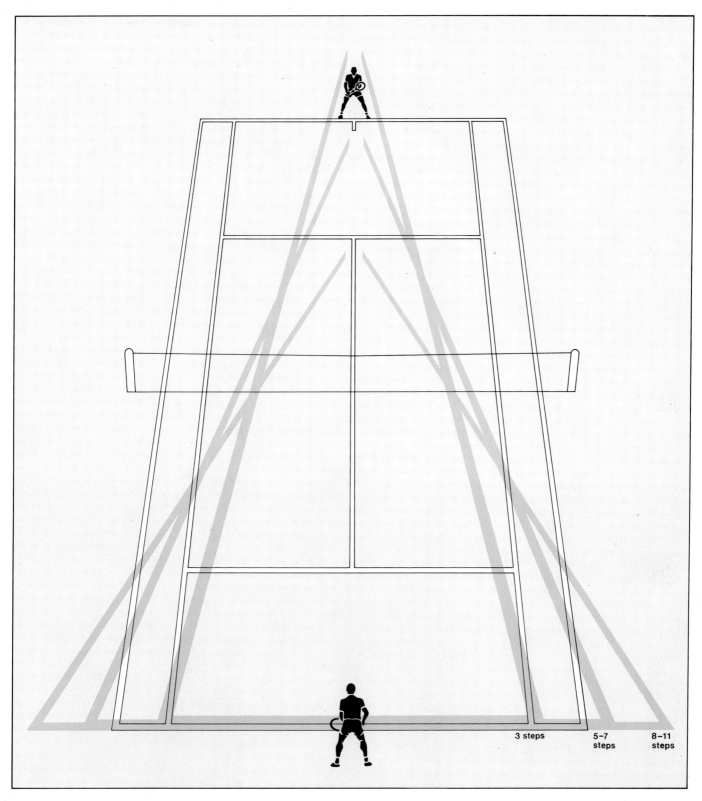

3 steps   5-7 steps   8-11 steps

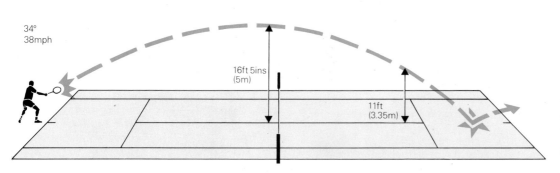

34°
38mph

16ft 5ins (5m)

11ft (3.35m)

If you can keep your opponent behind the baseline (above) you will have to do less running. The shorter the distance you hit the ball into your opponent's court, the more steps you will have to take to retrieve his return. This diagram shows how many steps you can expect to run laterally for different depths of shot.

Borg (left) shifts from foot to foot as he awaits service so that he is alert and ready. By the time his opponent serves, he is poised to receive in either direction. Borg, Connors and John McEnroe all have this invaluable gift for reading the ball early.

Bjorn Borg's two-handed (far left) topspin backhand is the best in the game. It is unusual in that he employs more wrist than most players, but he still achieves unbelievable accuracy and consistency. He stays over the ball and watches it like a hawk descending on its prey. Few players watch the ball as closely as Bjorn. His concentration is extraordinary: an object lesson for every player.

Jimmy Connors (above) hits the finest example of the two-handed flat backhand. He takes more risks than Borg because he hits flatter, but he possesses an amazing degree of accuracy considering the power with which he strikes the ball. His stroke preparation is immaculate. Jimmy's knees are always bent, which means he is invariably in position, ready to go.

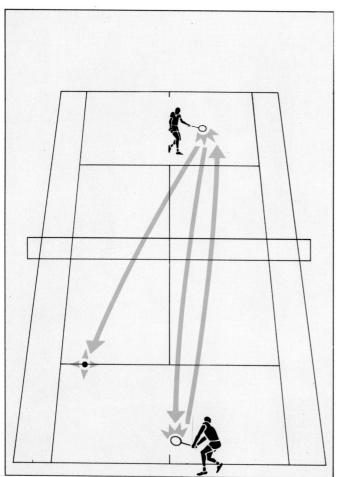

an imaginative new look at yourself, and changing your goals from negative to positive.

End of lesson in Psycho-Cybernetics. For more, read Dr Maltz! My point is that his guide to living can also be an excellent aid to the approach of a tennis player. Attitude is just as important as technique on a tennis court. So before you go out to play in a match you want to win, be sure to fill your mind with the right kind of thoughts. And if you are changing a defeatist self-image at the same time, so much the better.

Learn about yourself
It can be enormous fun learning about yourself on court, and I am not just talking about the professionals who find out in the hardest school of all. I mean for any players who fight their own private battles in the comparative obscurity of their club. When you have played a few long matches, had a few arguments, survived a few match points and come through a marathon deciding set, you are developing both as a competitor and as a person.

Tennis can teach you how to endure and survive, how to meet a crisis head on, face up to difficulties and come up smiling. It can be a measuring stick for other areas of your life. And the main lesson in tennis is, like the main lesson of life: never give up

fighting no matter how dismal the outlook or how big a hole you are in.

Tennis has given me confidence in myself. I own something that I know I have developed into a highly skilled craft. I've put in the time, achieved certain goals and found a great deal of self-satisfaction. I notice that I do not think of the past very much, which is healthy. I keep going and I really do believe that the best is yet to come.

What does winning mean?
Which is more important, winning or just playing? The question is often asked and of course the answer is that the two are intertwined. Winning can have different definitions for each individual. To some people, winning is giving 100 per cent. Even if they lose, so long as they have done their best they are satisfied—and why not? To others, winning means victory as represented by the score.

Winning is important to me because I know the price I have to pay in my lifestyle and routine. When I am working out twice a day till my eyeballs pop, and lifting weights every other day, I am paying what I consider to be a huge price in time and emotional investment. Winning becomes much more dear to me. My expectations would not be so high if I did not make such

On this spread and throughout the chapter, diagrams are used to illustrate how the top players execute their winning shots.

Bjorn Borg (above left) pounded the forehand of Jimmy Connors in the 1978 Wimbledon final but on this occasion his double handed backhand was too short and he left a glaring gap for Jimmy to exploit.

A flashback to Wimbledon (above), 1977 with Stan Smith, well placed at the net, not doing enough with his volley and giving Jimmy Connors a chance to pass him with a cross court forehand.

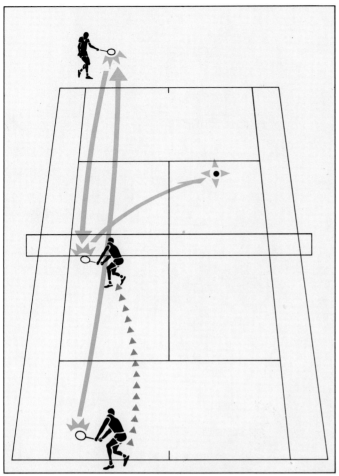

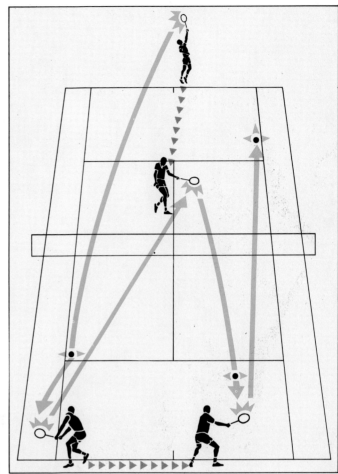

Bjorn Borg (above) wins most of his matches from the back of the court but his trips to the net are well timed and usually effective. Jimmy Connors went down the line in this 1978 Wimbledon rally but Borg surprised him with a sharply angled backhand volley.

Bjorn Borg (above right) needed all his speed of thought and movement to win this point against Roscoe Tanner in their 1979 Wimbledon final. Tanner's first volley was not deep enough and gave Borg the time and space he needed to end the rally.

This time Jimmy Connors (right) tried to deceive Bjorn Borg with a short, acutely angled forehand during their 1978 clash but Borg anticipated the move and wrapped up the point with a double handed backhand winner.

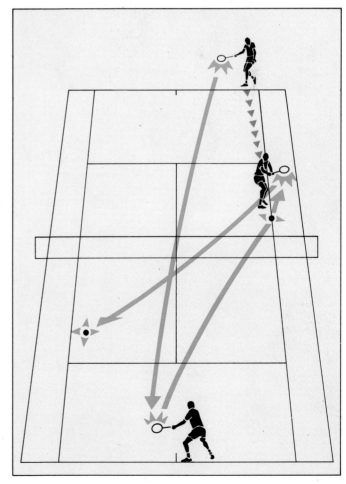

Left: This picture indicates the power of Martina's backhand volley. She is a strong and athletic player who rarely wastes an opportunity to get to the net and put the ball away. Notice how Martina leans into the volley from a sideways position. She turns her shoulder into the shot as she hits the ball well in front of her body.

Above: The best part of Chris Evert-Lloyd's game is her preparation and footwork. She never wastes a step and always has time to make the shot. Chris has the skill to hit crosscourt or down the line and the patience to wait for the opening she wants. She has tremendous accuracy, excellent anticipation and exemplary concentration. The only way to beat Chris is to try to make her run or take over at the net.

Right: Martina's serve is one of the best in the women's game. Being a left-hander, she is particularly dangerous when serving to the left court. The swinging ball takes the receiver way out of court and the return invites the deadly first volley.

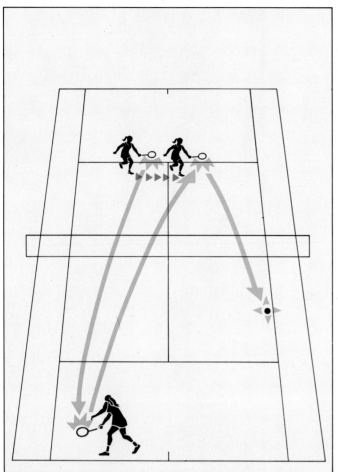
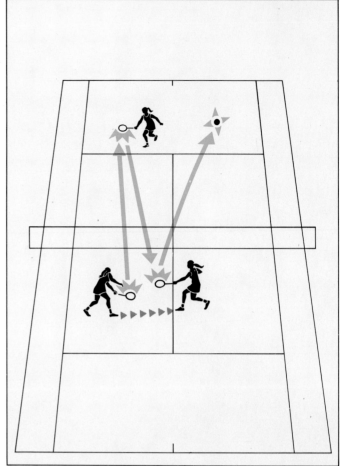

a heavy investment in success. I know that how well I play at Wimbledon is decided by how hard I practise and train in the months before the tournament. You are living in the now, but thinking of the future.

Work on your weaknesses
At a lower level, a player who wants to do well in the club championships should adopt a similar, if less arduous, programme. I don't care how small the event is, it still doesn't hurt to look forward, plan ahead and work on your weaknesses. If you are going to iron out a flaw in your backhand, give yourself six months to do it in— don't decide on the eve of the tournament.

You will not win all the time but the law of averages says you will win some of the time and find pleasure most of the time with the right sort of preparation. You must put the hours in, and always remember that it is never too late to improve. My forehand is much better at 36 than it was at 35. I wish I had learned the forehand I am using now when I was a kid. That is something I have learned as I have grown older.

There is always something to adapt in your game as the years go by. If you cannot run as well as you could, then improve your strokes or keep trying to run that bit faster; or improve your eye. Work out the

best way to adapt for you. Some of our over-70 players in the United States are marvellous examples of the standards that can be achieved even though you are elderly.

Keep improving
Never make the mistake of assuming that because you have a good stroke it is always going to be good. That is lazy thinking, not positive thinking. A strong shot is a bread-and-butter stroke, and something that you want to keep. If you don't want to lose it, don't neglect it by becoming obsessed with correcting a flaw in a weaker stroke. Even a reliable stroke needs practice.

When you are working on a weakness make sure that you have a sense of direction. Let us say that you feel your backhand is not as strong as it should be. You should ask yourself how is it weak: is it my stance, am I taking the racket back too late, or hitting the ball in the wrong place? And someone who is a really good teacher can tell you how to make it right, not just what is wrong.

That is a positive reaction again. Incidentally, I hope this book will enable players to teach themselves to a certain degree. I believe that being a successful teacher involves making your pupils more independent, not more dependent. Too many coaches make their students too dependent

Martina Navratilova's volleying (above left) was a vital factor in winning the first of her Wimbledon titles in 1978. This is a typical exchange during her semi-final victory over Evonne Cawley. Evonne gets to the first volley but Martina punches the second one away.

Martina Navratilova (above) had to fire a backhand and a forehand volley before she won this match of her quarter final against Betty Stove when Wimbledon celebrated its centenary in 1977. It illustrates her quick thinking mobility, but on this occasion she lost the match.

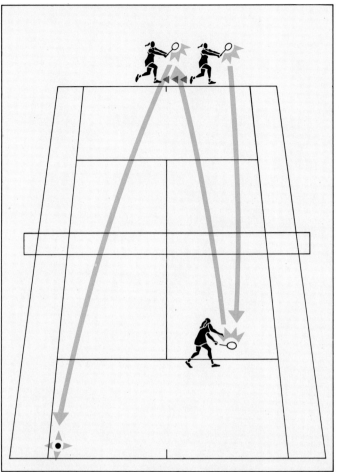

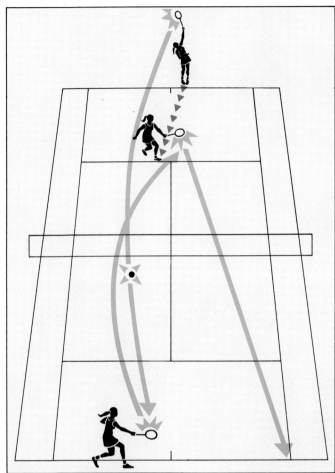

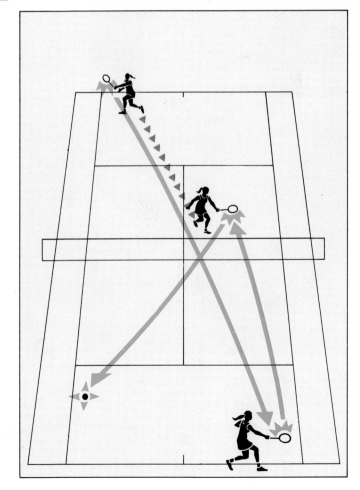

Only the best volleys (above) disturb the immaculate ground strokes of Chris Evert-Lloyd. Although she was beaten by Martina Navratilova in the 1978 Wimbledon final her double handed backhand was a model of control and accuracy.

A typical Navratilova one-two (above right) ended her 1978 Wimbledon final against Chris Evert-Lloyd. Martina served, came in and volleyed the return hard and deep to the corner of the court.

Another clip (right) from that 1978 Wimbledon final. Martina races in behind a cross court backhand drive and meets Chris's forehand with a perfectly angled forehand volley.

The natural successor to Chris Evert-Lloyd as far as style is concerned is Tracy Austin. She is exactly like Chris except that she is willing to go to the net more. Tracy is a better player at her age than Chris was, But this reflects the fact that the level of play in the women's game is higher at every age. Like Chris, she has excellent footwork and preparation. She will be around for a long time.

Sue Barker's forehand is a lethal weapon—her bread-and-butter shot and one of the best forehands in the women's game when it is working well. She goes for it full out. There is no compromise. Sue also moves very well.

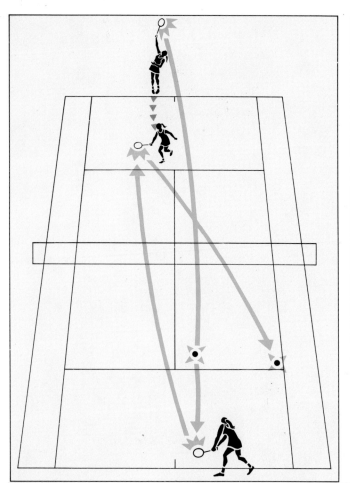

on them for advice and guidance. That is bad because players are apt to stop thinking for themselves.

Overcome negative attitudes

Tennis is a game of the mind, and because of that you hear a lot about 'choking' or 'getting the elbow'. The terms are part of the game's vocabulary. Choking means that everything breaks down when you are under pressure, like pressing the accelerator in a car and going no place. Your co-ordination is strangled and everything shuts down. The elbow means that your arm suddenly feels as though it is encased in cement. I call it Tight City. Don't ask me why, that's just my phrase for a frame of mind which afflicts all tennis players at some stage. It is a built-in fear of something that has not happened but looks as though it will.

The only way to cure it is by strength of mind, that positive approach which is so terribly important. Play for the moment and not for what might happen later in the match. Build up a mental picture of the next shot going in. What your brain is made to imagine is what you will feel in the rest of your body. Keep your expectations high and you can really stay loose and live up to your highest hopes. Expect the worst and it often happens.

How you react on court

Sometimes it helps to be exactly the opposite to your normal self when you are playing. Before a big tournament like Wimbledon I keep thinking about bad line calls and picture myself reacting in a way which is completely at variance with my normal, extrovert manner. I visualize myself keeping quiet and just carrying on with the next point. If I reach boiling point then I have to get rid of it quickly and get back to the task in hand. But advance thinking like that does prepare you for crises, and gives you a chance to discipline your reaction.

There are two sides to the coin, of course. More docile human beings than me should programme themselves into a frame of mind where they are prepared to stand up for their rights. Just because you are reserved and shy does not mean that you should allow yourself to be trampled on left, right and centre.

You might be the meekest player of all time but if you are in a club match without an umpire and you are getting cheated, don't take it. You can be courteous as well as assertive. Ask yourself if you would let 10 people jump in front of you in a queue. Of course not. So don't be shoved around on a tennis court. Be firm, take positive action and say hello to the new, gutsy you!

Virginia Wade (above left) hit some inspired volleys during her 1977 title winning triumph over Chris Evert-Lloyd at Wimbledon. This is one of them: a deep serve to Chris's backhand followed by a firm, well placed volley.

Tracy Austin's double handed backhand (above) is one of the most reliable in the game. Martina Navratilova made the mistake of volleying to it twice in this rally during their 1979 Wimbledon semi-final, and was passed.

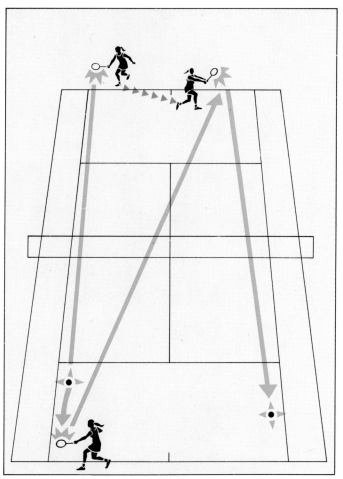

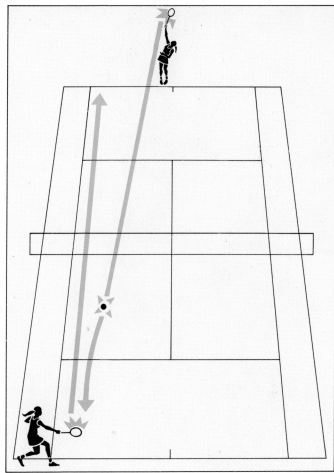

Austin's double hander again (above). Martina tests her with a cross court forehand drive but Tracy wins the point with one of her favourite shots, a backhand down the line. (Note: Tracy lost the match!)

Many players would have returned this Pam Shriver service (above right) on the backhand but in this excerpt from a 1978 Wimbledon match Sue Barker moves to the left and detonates her explosive forehand to fire a winner down the line.

This is (right) a 1977 Wimbledon exchange of backhands between players more notable for their forehand expertise: Sue Barker and Kerry Reid. Sue often runs round her backhand but on this occasion she resisted the temptation and hit a winner from her weaker side.

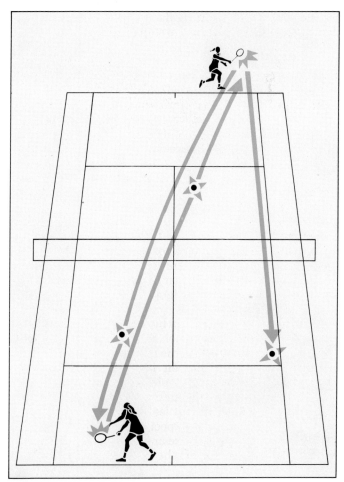

Strategy

Patterns • Targets
Serving • Singles
Doubles • Partners
Mixed Doubles
Competition
Formations
Positions

Singles: tactical thinking

Plan important matches beforehand by preparing a game plan. Learn and digest all you can about your opponent's strengths and weaknesses. Treat each point as a separate entity and never assume you are going to win no matter how dominant your position.

The longer I play tennis the more convinced I become that the whole secret of the game is living in the now. By this I mean developing an outlook in which each point is isolated from the rest. The state of the match should be irrelevant to the moment. Even match point becomes just another point if you observe the right sort of discipline.

It is difficult to acquire this detached approach because it is so easy to get carried away by the ebb and flow of a match. Tension and excitement can cut your concentration to shreds. A match I lost to Nancy Richey at Madison Square Garden in 1978 was a classic example of this. I will never forget what was one of my worst moments in tennis.

Don't anticipate a win
There was intense rivalry between Nancy and me at the time, although curiously enough we had not played each other for over three years. The last time we had met was in the quarter-finals at Forest Hills, and she won. I had just signed a professional contract, and I wanted to beat her so badly I became unbelievably tense. After all, I was supposed to the best woman player in the world.

I won the first set and at 5–3 in the second I reached match point. Then I was faced with this lob from Nancy which was so easy it was untrue. I had all the time in the world to put it away but after changing my mind about three times I finally managed a sort of overhead which landed about

a foot out. And that was that. I failed to win another game. Nancy won the third set 6–0 and I had been humiliated before a crowd of 10,000 people.

Rod Laver came up to me and said, 'Don't worry, you always have two or three of those in your lifetime. That's life.' But the moral of the story was one I have never forgotten. I played the point badly because it was match point. The fact that it was the shot which should have ended the contest contributed to the awful goof which changed the direction of the whole match.

I had not been living in the now. I was already thinking of victory, the happiness, the cheers of the audience. Everything, in fact, but the comparatively simple job of putting away that vital smash. Helen Jacobs once endured a similar fate against her arch rival Helen Wills Moody at Wimbledon. Many years later at the Garden I knew how she had felt.

The same sort of thing happened to me in reverse towards the end of 1979. I was playing Betty Stove in the final at Stockholm and I had double-faulted to put Betty 5–4 up in the final set. She had me, and she should have won. But she began to think 'I can win this match' and in her own mind she was already four points ahead, and shaking hands at the net. Betty lost her concentration and blew the match, which I won 6–3 6–7 7–5. She had fallen into the oldest tennis trap of all: savouring a victory before it had happened.

I like to think I have learned my lesson, although you can never afford to be com-

Don't suddenly start to serve harder merely because you are serving for victory. Just flood your mind with thoughts of where you are going to put your first serve. And never fall victim to complacency. Bottle up that sigh of relief and feeling of joy until the match is over. It is worth waiting for.

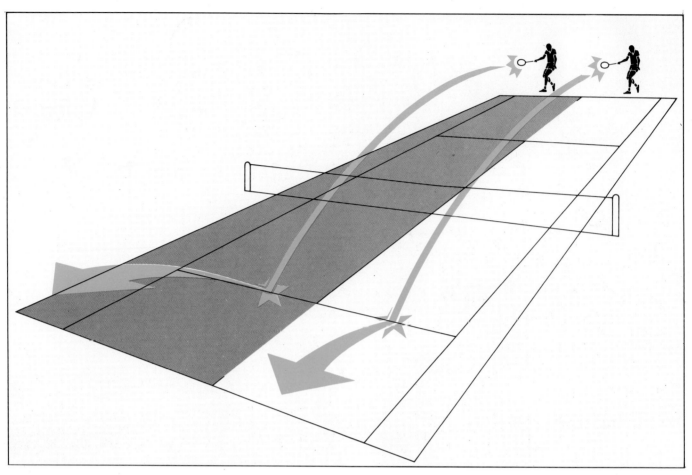

placent. When you are so close to success your pulse rate soars and it is hard to resist the temptation to go one jump ahead of reality. Nowadays, when I get into a position like that I fight this mental battle in which I tell myself to come back to *now*, and play each point as a separate entity.

Serving for victory
When you are serving for victory all you should be doing is filling your mind with thoughts of where you are going to put your first serve. And my advice to the average player serving at that stage is continue whatever you have been doing to get yourself in a match winning position. Don't suddenly try to hit the ball harder because you have one foot in the door of victory.

It is a debatable point who is under more pressure in a game which could be the last of a match. Theoretically, it should be the receiver because the server has the initiative. But if the server is inhibited by the situation, the pressure can be reversed. So just play each point for what it is worth. Save that sigh of relief, that feeling of exhilaration, until it is all over.

Work out the target area
I think steadiness is something every club player ought to aim for. If you can get the ball back a few extra times you will win more matches than most of your rivals at

the club, and to do this you should try to build a mental picture of a target area to aim at on the opposite baseline.

The width of this area should be about 6 ft (2 m) either side of the centre line, and its depth should be about 12 ft (4 m). If you can keep the ball in that area consistently I guarantee that you will start to win a lot more points. By hitting the ball deep down the middle you are depriving your opponent of angles and tempting him or her to make mistakes as you build up your own rhythm and confidence.

By all means hit crosscourt when the right moment arrives, but the crosscourt drive is creating more area for the return so make sure you find a good angle and a firm stroke when you stop hitting deep down the middle. Learn to be patient, spar for the opening, and then use it!

Prepare a game plan
It is a good idea to prepare a game plan before you go into an important match. You must have a clue what you are going to do before you walk out on court, so try to watch your opponent beforehand and give some time and thought to how you are going to play your match. Give yourself a sense of purpose and direction by thinking about it the night before, not as you are driving to the club on the afternoon of the contest.

Generally speaking, the ball does not bounce as high on a fast court and it carries further. Clay puts a brake on the ball. It means a higher bounce (above left) and longer rallies. Patience is a distinct virtue on clay, where you have to really work for points and nothing is easily gained. Big servers with hard ground strokes who are anxious to end a rally as quickly as possible feel happier on faster surfaces. On grass the bounce is low and usually fast (above right) although Wimbledon seems to be getting slower these days. A good grass court is nice but there are not too many of them left. One of the drawbacks is the inconsistency of the bounce, but grass is certainly easier on the feet. Cement can be fast or slow depending on the texture of the top surface. Synthetic surfaces used indoors can also vary in speed according to the ingredients from which they are made. My favourite court is Supreme because it is a versatile surface to play on.

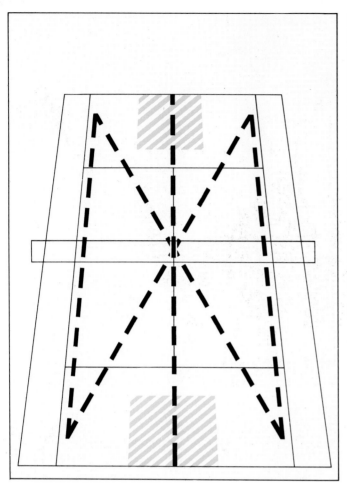

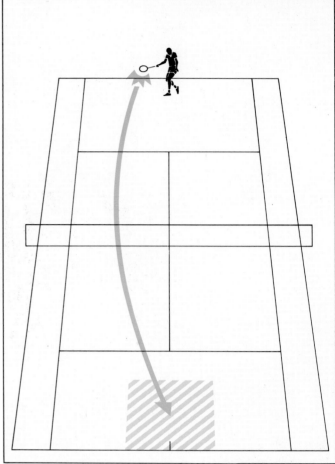

Make a mental note of how your opponent reacts to different types of strokes. Which is his or her favourite passing shot, down the line or across the court? Are you in for a lot of lobbing, or are you going to be dealing with a determined net rusher? Is the serve a threat? Are there any glaring weaknesses?

Finding the answers to questions like these will at least send you into the match with a rough idea of what to do. Incidentally, although it is common sense to exploit a weakness, never forget that constant attention to a flaw in a player's armoury can turn that weakness into a strength.

Bill Tilden tried to break down his opponent's strength first—and sometimes that is a good idea although what succeeded for a genius like Tilden does not always work with ordinary mortals. Don't be rushed into anything. Hit deep down the middle for the first few games to build up your consistency and confidence, and then you can move on from there.

Vary your strokes

Once you have got the feel of the ball, it is a good idea to keep your opponent guessing by varying your stroke pattern. Make it obvious that your mind is alert and that you are thinking your way through the rallies, not merely going through the motions.

Getting out of a tight spot

Always be ready to scramble. Many close matches have been won by a few desperate, ungainly lunges which you will never find in any tennis manual. No game can be played exactly to the book: that's for practice. When you are out there competing, all you should be trying to do is to focus on the ball and get it back.

Some days you are going to play a lot better than others, but whether your strokes are creaking or not, always make sure that you get to as many balls as you can. Never stop running and don't let style dominate your thoughts. If you are in a tight spot you cannot be graceful or poised. Just forget your dignity, chase that ball and hope you can get your racket to it. You will be surprised how many times you can turn an apparently hopeless situation into a winning point.

Change a losing game

What if your plan goes wrong? One of the oldest rules of tennis is, always change a losing game. This is not easy but, rather than submit meekly to whatever punishment your opponent is inflicting on you, try something different. If you have been playing defensively, introduce a spot of offence. A little adventurous aggression is rarely wasted and it could dent the confidence of

A typical warm up routine for many of us is to hit a series of deep cross court drives. Make a goal, like 10 or 20 shots in a row, preferably landing near the baseline (above left). Repeat the process down the line or down the middle with both forehand and backhand. Always try to have lots of balls to maintain continuity. It is important to remember that practice should involve moving up and back as well as from side to side.

Every club player ought to strive for steadiness. Try to build a mental picture of a target area in the middle of the opposite baseline (above). Hitting the ball deep down the middle into this area will deprive your opponent of angles and tempt him into making mistakes.

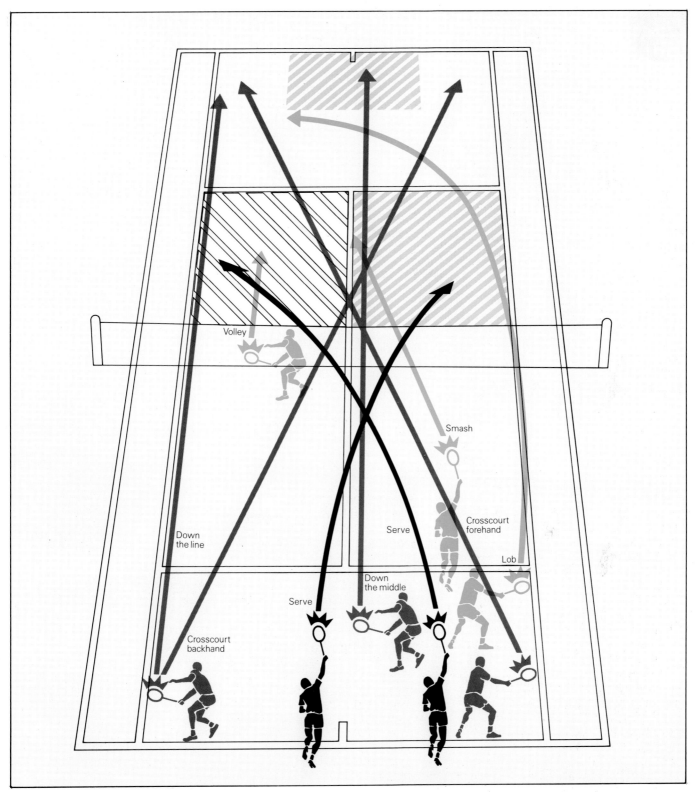

Volley

Smash

Crosscourt
forehand

Serve

Lob

Down
the line

Down
the middle

Serve

Crosscourt
backhand

All the shots you need are
explained in this diagram,
together with the
terminology.

your rival. Another way of putting the brake on a match which is rushing away from you is to vary the speed and spin of your returns to break up the tempo of the rallies.

Think of alternatives. Try to be aware of why you are losing and ask yourself questions like 'Am I being too aggressive?' or 'Am I being too defensive?'. Perhaps too much reliance on aggression is making you erratic, or maybe you are just not feeling

that ball. Aim at keeping the ball in play by hitting down the middle until you find your rhythm and consistency. Of course there are times when no matter what you do your opponent is going to be too good! The moral is keep trying. You never know when the player on the other side of the net is going to lose his touch.

Never forget that the person you are playing is going through the same mental and physical turmoil as yourself. You are

Arthur Ashe has been a
great ambassador for
tennis through the years.
He had to retire for health
reasons but hopefully he
will go on contributing to
the game in other ways.
He will always be
remembered for a
marvellous tactical
triumph over Jimmy
Connors (left) in the 1975
Wimbledon final. He was a
strong and spectacular
player with a magnificent
serve and an explosive
backhand.

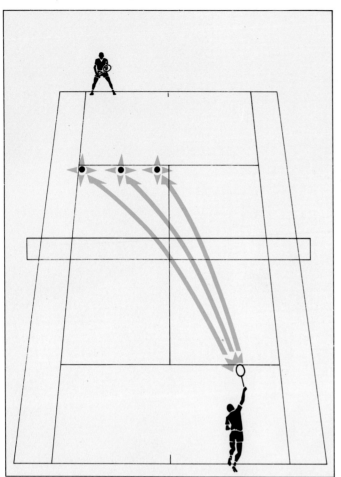
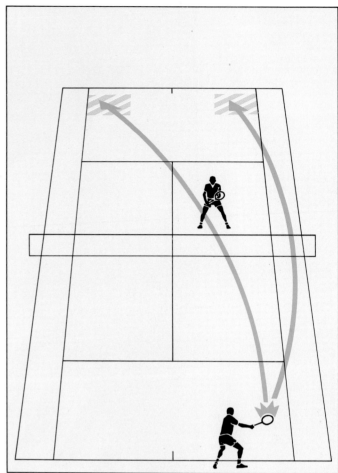

not on your own as you try to fight off anxiety, frustration and maybe exhaustion. Strength of mind can be decisive, so hang in there. Focus on the ball and by concentrating hard give each point an identity of its own.

Stay competitive

Be competitive. Keep thinking. Try not to reach a frame of mind where a match has become a matter of going through the motions. A resigned acceptance of defeat will boost your opponent's morale even further, and give you the air of a born loser.

Never forget the score. If you do it is usually a sign that you are not concentrating or, even worse, don't care who wins. Always make sure that the score is in no doubt, particularly in a match where the players are doing the calling. There is nothing more irritating, time consuming or ruinous to concentration than repeated stoppages to discuss the score.

I have stressed the necessity to play each point for what it is worth but it goes without saying that some points are more important than others—and I don't just mean the points that end games. All the points from 30–15 onwards are vital. Winning the point at 30–15 can give you two chances of grabbing the game, whereas losing it will prolong the agony.

Try to exploit your opponent's weakness when you are serving (above left). This is usually the backhand but just for variety throw in a slice to the forehand or—to add to the confusion—fire some balls directly at his body. The moral is never to let the receiver settle into a groove. Keep him guessing with speed, spin and placement.

Aggression or caution?

As a general rule, if you are ahead—say, 40–0 or 40–15—be aggressive. Take a chance, because the bulk of the pressure is on your opponent. Being down by a similar margin calls for a little more caution: nothing defeatist, just enough care to make your rival earn the game and not receive it as a present.

Avoid drop shots, stop volleys and risky angles on pressure points. They look terrific when they come off but they are a costly embarrassment when they end in disaster. The anguish when one fails is often so lingering that it can cost you the next point as well.

Lobbing from corner to corner (above) makes sense because it gives you more court to aim at and reduces the possibility of hitting out while increasing your chances of making a shot which is not only high but deep. But for maximum effect, lob to your opponent's backhand. Even if the ball is returned it will usually be weak.

You must get as close to the net as possible for the first volley (above right) because hopefully you will end the rally with it and the nearer you are to the net the more options are open to you. Follow the path of your serve as you go in. Advance as far as you can and try to hit the ball before it starts to drop. Usually you will find yourself in the volleying zone shown here, but if you can move further in, do so.

If you are lucky enough to get a high return the general rule is to volley it across the court (above far right). If the ball is dipping to your shoe tops, you should hit it in front of you or down the line and then get in position for the next volley.

Billie Jean King putting away a thunderous volley (right) during a match in Australia.

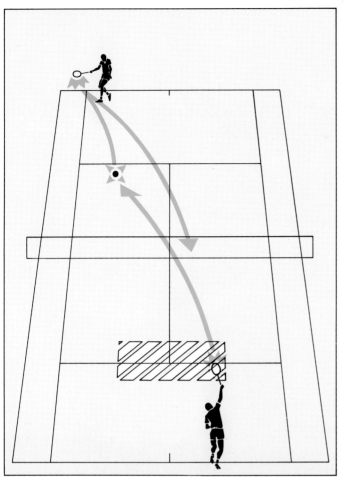

Doubles: sharing the load

How to get the most out of doubles, the game which is most played at club level. It demands touch, imagination and above all teamwork. Find a partner you can communicate with and work together. And forget about the weaker sex when you are playing mixed!

Most club players play a lot more doubles than singles. There are several reasons for this. One is that doubles is more social than singles. Another is that it is not quite as energetic because you are covering only a quarter of the court instead of half of it. The load is shared between you and your partner.

But maybe the most important factor is that doubles is such a wonderfully stimulating game, involving imagination, creativity, touch and teamwork. There are few aspects of tennis to equal the excitement of a well-played doubles rally which brings out the best in both partnerships.

You and your partner

I believe that the number one necessity in a doubles team is that you should like each other, or at least have an understanding, a sense of communication while you are out there. The French call it rapport. Without it, doubles is not half the fun and doesn't provide half the incentive to do well. Doubles partners don't have to be the best of friends off court, but on court they should be able to speak and feel relaxed with each other.

I've been fortunate in the quality of partner I've had in my career. I won two Wimbledon titles with Karen Susman, one with Maria Bueno, one with Betty Stove, one with Martina Navratilova, and five with Rosie Casals. I got along with all of them although the two easiest in terms of being on the same mental wavelength were Martina and Karen. We never had harsh words, always understood what we were

There is a lot of give and take in doubles play, which is why the top priority in a pair must be a feeling of mutual respect and understanding. Here, Martina Navratilova and I are taking charge of the forecourt, where most doubles rallies are decided.

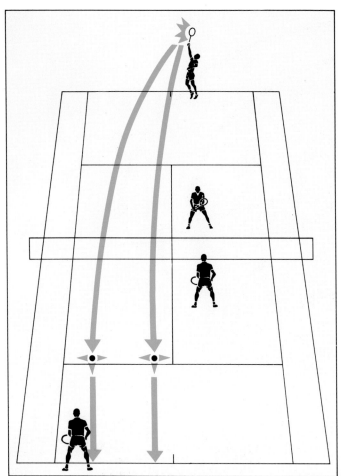

doing, and we laughed a lot.

Rosie and I had a lot of highs and lows but at Wimbledon in 1967, 1968, 1970, 1971 and 1973 we really got our act together. That's when we were firing on all cylinders as a team. I would say I had my highest moments in doubles with Rosie, but also some of my lowest. We are different people and we have a hard time communicating sometimes. She's always late, and I have this thing about being on time. Rosie is not all that keen on practice but I am because I think that preparation is everything if I decide to go for something.

Working together

Good communication is reflected in the efficiency of the calling. It should be almost instinctive—a kind of sixth sense, but some players are quicker than others at calling 'Mine' or 'Yours'. For instance, I had to do a lot of adjusting with Rosie because she could never call quickly. She invariably called late. It was something we talked about, and there was no friction. But it was a problem. Sometimes you need to know whether to go for a shot, or back off because your partner is going to take it.

There is no doubt that Rosie had problems with me too—including my volatile temper. Sometimes the perfectionist in me made me too demanding on myself, and this rebounded on Rosie. But these are problems you have to be ready to handle as a doubles team—and our record shows that we coped.

Partners should be able to ease the pressure on each other. Martina was so anxious to help me win that record twentieth Wimbledon title when we played doubles in 1979 that she made herself a wreck. She was so nervous she could hardly breathe— yet only the day before she had won the singles title for the second successive year! I felt fine at the start of the final, but when her nerves began getting through to me I decided to joke around a bit when we changed sides. 'You know, this isn't my last Wimbledon, Martina,' I said, 'I know you keep thinking it is but in case we don't win today, it's OK. I'm going to be back next year.' Martina discovered how to smile again, and became more like her true self.

That sort of thing would not work with everybody. Certain people do not want to talk on court because it makes them lose their concentration. Others appreciate a bit of encouraging chat. One good rule, if something is not going right, is to say 'Why don't *we* try to do this'. Always 'we', never 'you', even if your partner is the weak link at the time. Remember that you are in the match as one unit, not two. Your aim should be to build up each other's morale.

The tandem, or Australian formation (above left) in which the server's partner adopts a net position on the same side as the server to block the cross court return often pays dividends. It is particularly effective against a receiver who has a flair for returning cross court from the backhand but is not so good at returning down the line. The more traditional formation (above) shows the partner in the opposite court.

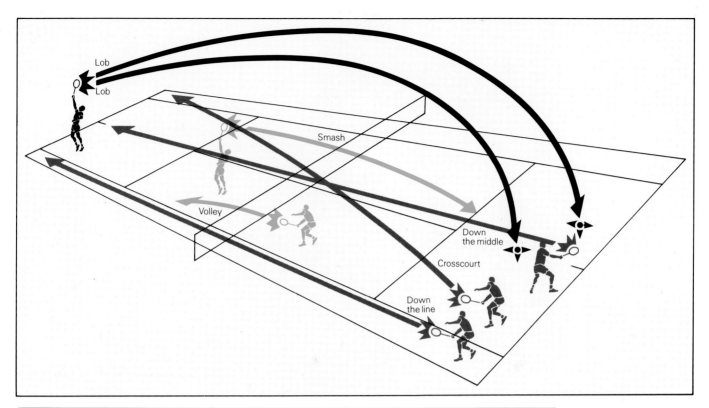

Lob
Lob
Smash
Volley
Down the middle
Crosscourt
Down the line

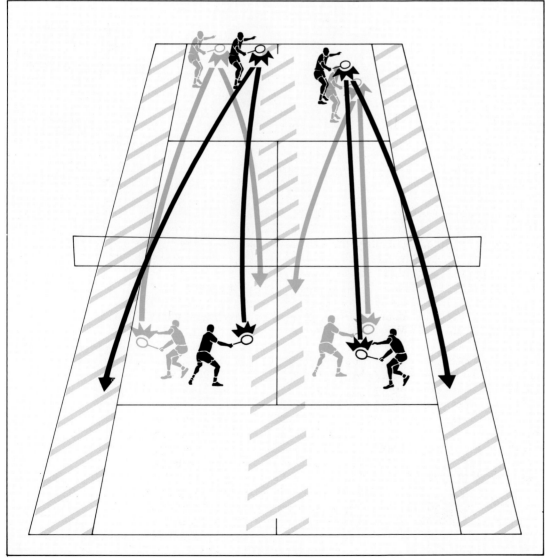

Always remember to use your full range of strokes (above) and the increased width of the court, when playing doubles.

First of all, in doubles play, it is imperative that you get on with your partner. There must be good vibrations both on and off the court, otherwise the team will not work. The first rule of doubles play is to take control of the net, and doubles partners must work together to achieve this. Try to force your opponents to hit up. Unless you have an obvious put-away, hit down the middle of the court (left). Similarly, when in doubt aim down the centre.

I have played on both sides of the court in doubles and believe that the forehand court is the more difficult because of its demands on touch and variation. Many people argue that the left court or backhand player is the dominant partner as so many vital points are played from that side. But the right court player has big points too—30-all for example—and he must be ready to produce a backhand down the middle, although this one brought a look of apprehension to the face of my partner, Betty Stove.

There must be a big element of give and take in doubles. Sometimes you are the leader of the team; sometimes you have to be content with a supporting part. Roles change even within a point because good partners are always trying to set up the ball for one another. Nobody plays the hero all the time in a successful doubles combination.

The dominant partner
It is often said that the backhand, or left court, player is the dominant figure in any doubles team. This is true to a certain degree because in a close game the vital points are played from that court. But there is a great deal of pressure on the player in the right, or forehand, court as well.

The first point of a game is extremely important and this, of course, involves the right court player. The 30-all point is another heavy one because it can relieve or increase the pressure on the left court player in the next rally. I've played on both sides and I have found that the forehand court is the more difficult because it demands greater touch and variation.

As well as returning with your forehand you have always to be ready to take serves down the centre of the court on your backhand. This calls for accuracy of the highest degree if you are to avoid the volleyer at the net. I call it threading the needle and it is another reason why I would never under-estimate the value of the player in the forehand court.

Mixed doubles
When it's good, there is nothing better than mixed doubles. It is an under-rated event, but it's the best going when played well. Some of my all-time great matches have been in the mixed. Again, you have got to think about team work, but this time of course there is the additional factor of having two men and two women on court. The old way of mixed doubles thinking was that the man took everything difficult but I don't think that applies today.

What is happening now is that women are pushing themselves harder and raising their expectations, not only in tennis but in life generally. There is no need to feel the weaker half of a partnership just because you are a woman. The man might be stronger, but he is not always the better player. And a quick-thinking woman can deal with any powerful shot directed at her by standing her ground and blocking the ball back.

The woman's role
Very often a woman's fear of taking the initiative in mixed doubles is all in the mind. She does not want to make a fool of

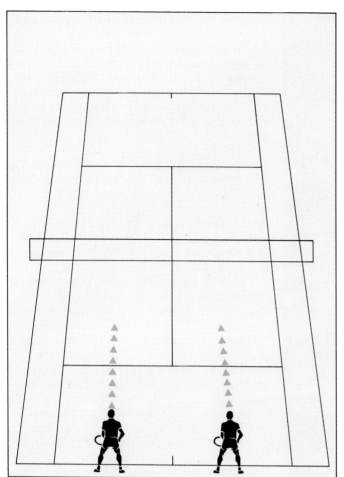

herself, and she allows this usually un-founded apprehension to inhibit her play, throwing added responsibility on the prob-ably reluctant shoulders of her partner. The best mixed doubles partnerships are be-tween equals, although I concede that it is best for the man to act as leader of the team.

Owen Davidson, and I won four Wimble-don mixed doubles titles. I always knew what Owen expected me to do. If there was a volley or a smash to take, I took it. He would have wondered what was happening if I had not done my job at the net or had left him all the overheads.

There is no reason for a man to feel over-protective of his woman partner in mixed doubles. In fact, I think a woman is embar-rassed in such a situation. If a woman wants to play mixed she must go out there and expect the ball to be hit as hard at her as it is at anyone else. That's part of the price one pays.

I know that if there's a set up in mixed I stand a good chance of getting it right in the gut. I realize that when I walk on court, so there is no point in turning every hot rally into a scene from *Swan Lake*. Women who play mixed should be ready for any situa-tions that arise and be prepared to prove that they are not as vulnerable as tradition suggests. They have to make their own way in a game.

Finding the right partner

Mixed doubles have ended many beautiful friendships and it is doubly important to find the right partner. Just because you are husband and wife does not mean to say that you are going to make it in mixed doubles. In fact, a marital partnership rarely makes an amicable mixed doubles team. My advice to husbands and wives is to stay on opposite sides of the net in mixed. In that way there are fewer chances of crises which might lead to domestic squabbles.

Doubles play

Many people make better doubles than singles players because they thrive on the thrust and counter-thrust produced by doubles: the angles, the reflex action vol-leys, the tactical manoeuvring and the swiftly changing pattern of the exchanges between four players all thirsting to put the ball away.

The forecourt is the area where most doubles rallies are decided. The pair who assume command of this part of the court stand the best chance of winning the point. That is why the server should follow his service to the net, and why the returner should also head for the net after making his return. Hectic, close-in volleying is a characteristic of doubles play.

You must be aggressive and assertive in

There should be an invisible bond between doubles partners (above left and right). If one goes to the net, the other should go too. If one retreats, the other should retreat as well. One-up one-back situations should be avoided wherever possible. If a player moves sideways, his partner should move the same way to avoid leaving a gap down the middle. Of course, there are occasions in the heat of a match when this pattern is broken up but always remember that the best doubles combinations work together, not separately. Unison is the name of the game.

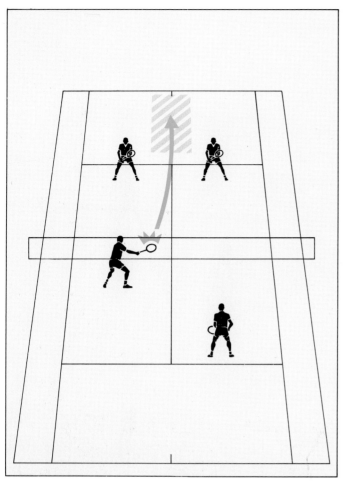

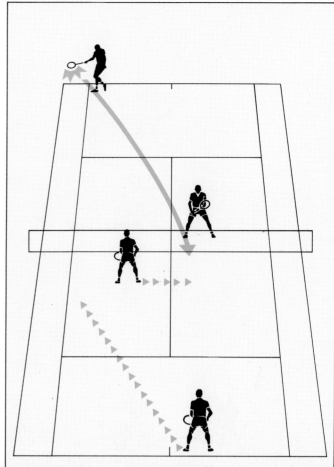

One of the wisest principles in doubles play is to hit down the middle of the court (above) as often as possible. Apart from shooting over the lowest part of the net, you are creating indecision in your opponents by placing the ball between them.

Don't leave gaps. If you are serving (above right) and your partner decides to cross over and intercept the return, make sure you move and cover the empty court. This plugging of loopholes is a vital part of the teamwork which characterizes every effective doubles pair.

In a one-up one-back situation (right) it is good tactics to volley behind the opposing net player as long as you are close enough to the net to put the ball away. Volleying directly to the player at the back of the court throws away the initiative and maybe the point.

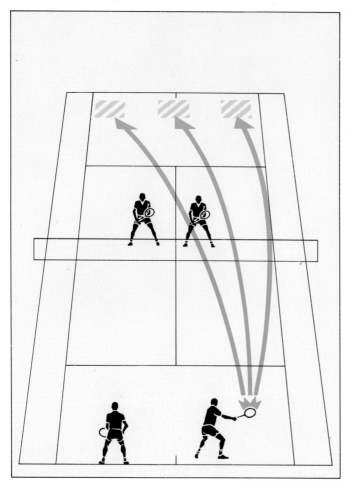

Right   Wrong

A typical doubles situation (above left). The opposition is at the net poised to end the rally with a volley. You and your partner are pinned to the baseline. A lob is often the best way to break an apparent stranglehold. It is usually more effective than attempting to hit a sharply angled drive, and will at least ease the pressure by pushing your rivals to the back of the court.

The basic return of service (left) in doubles is across the court. Apart from the occasional down-the-line drive to keep the net player 'honest', there is no point in presenting him with a volley. Go crosscourt, keeping the ball as far as possible from the player at the net and trying to make it pitch at the feet of the incoming server.

Serve deep (above) and get in as close to the net as possible. Try to reach a position level with your partner. You might not succeed but the thought will act aa a spur as you go in for that first volley. The back of the court is a no-man's land for the volleyer.

Being the woman in a mixed doubles partnership (right) does not mean that you should regard yourself as the weaker half. Although it is advisable for the man to act as leader of the team, the best mixed doubles combinations are between equals. Owen Davidson, with whom I won four Wimbledon mixed titles, would have been puzzled if I had not done my job at the net or overhead.

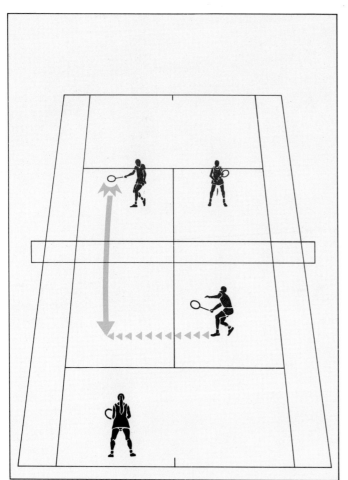

doubles. There is no future at all in staying back and allowing your opponents to set up volleying positions at the net. You must get in, and when you advance, go as a pair. A one-up and one-back formation is bad tactics.

The first shots

The most important shots in doubles are the serve, the service return and the first volley. This is the tense moment at the start of a rally which often decides the destiny of the point. A good return will dip to the incoming server's feet, forcing the server to volley up and open the way for a possible interception at the net. It is advisable to vary your returns, using topspin, the chip and sometimes the lob to upset the server's composure. Weak second serves should be treated mercilessly and returned as hard as accuracy permits.

I know that many club players are reluctant to follow their service in and volley. Perhaps they are not nimble enough or maybe their volley is not good enough. If that is the case wait for a return that pitches on the service line or in front of it, and then get in. Treat the net like a magnet and don't fight its attraction. It's the best place to be in doubles.

Return serve crosscourt more often than not, although it is not a bad idea to start a match by firing a few returns down the line just to remind the sharp shooting volleyer at the net that it is not always safe to cross over for attempted interceptions. It takes courage and control but at least the receiver is showing that he is not easy prey for the poacher.

The tandem formation

Variants are recommended to add spice and surprise to doubles strategy. The tandem or Australian formation, in which the server's partner takes up a net position on the same side as the server to cut off the crosscourt return, can be a smart move, particularly against a left-hander in the backhand court. And don't be afraid to stand back and lob if you are going through a period of heavy pressure from the net. Lobbing gives you time to collect your wits and sends the volleyer back to the baseline.

Serving

Service speed is not imperative in doubles. In fact, it is often wiser to shut down on the power in favour of control and depth. A spun service deep in the box is just as effective as a powerhouse delivery. Look at Frankie Durr, one of the finest women's doubles players of recent years. She served at about two miles an hour but looped it in deep and was able to follow it in as well.

For the man: DON'T be a court hog (above left) because you will get yourself out of position too often, to the embarrassment of yourself and your partner. If you want to use the whole court you might as well play singles. DO have some confidence in your partner, (above) otherwise neither of you is going to have any fun.

For the woman: DON'T expect to be shielded (above). You are out there to play doubles and to fill an equal role in the rallies. DO accept your share of volleying (above right) and smashing. Hold your ground. Doubles is doubles, whether it is men's, women's or mixed. If you appear to be the weaker person you will be a target, so be ready to play your part to the full. If there is a choice and it is to your partner's strength, let him *or* her take it.

Make this your objective rather than sheer strength when you are serving in doubles.

Generally speaking, it is a sound idea to serve at the receiver's backhand because that is usually the weaker side. But do not let your serving fall into a too predictable routine. Ring the changes in direction, spin and pace to keep the receiver guessing. The odd moment of hesitation is often the preliminary to winning the point.

Placing the ball

Doubles involves using the full dimensions of the court and sometimes it is tempting to exploit that additional width by going for the alley, or sidelines. Of course, that extra breadth should not be ignored, but one of the great maxims of doubles play is to hit down the middle as often as possible.

Why? First, in shooting down the middle you are hitting the ball over the lowest part of the net. Second, the ball has a better chance of landing in court. Third, you are creating indecision in your opponents by placing the ball between them. They have to decide who is going to take the next shot, and that split second of uncertainty can be crucial. With a little bit of luck they might both leave the return to each other, with the result that nobody goes for it.

A fourth reason is the one I mentioned in the chapter about singles play. A shot down

the middle creates the least scope for an angled return. My advice in doubles is, play the percentages by going down the centre, and reap the dividends.

Who plays where?

Because the best doubles teams aim their attack down the middle, a question mark is raised over the belief that the player with the best forehand should play in the right court and the player with the strongest backhand should play in the left court.

This leaves the two sides of the court protected but what about the centre, the solar plexus? Is it safe for it to be covered by the two weakest shots of the players concerned? Maybe not. Sometimes it is smart for your two most reliable shots to be used to cope with problems in the middle, and this can mean a switching of courts. It is certainly worth discussing if you have a partner with whom you want to build up a successful relationship in doubles.

Finally, one of the secrets of good doubles play is keeping the ball low when you return it into the opposite court (apart from lobs, of course). High returns give your opponents a better chance of firing the ball back for a winner or at least producing a shot which spells pressure. Aim for low returns which force the recipient to hit up and give you the opportunity to hit down.

Strokes

**Contact • Forehand • Backhand
Serving • Volley • Smash • Lob**

Making contact

The most graceful swing in the business is not much use if the racket does not hit the ball in the right place at the right moment. Think about the point of contact and sooner or later the rest will come naturally.

This is just a brief note about an area of tennis which is often submerged in the Niagara of words which have spilled over the subject since experts started trying to advise people on the best way to play the game. It is the place where the racket face meets the ball: the point of contact, or the strike zone, call it what you will.

Of course, ground strokes don't mean a thing if they haven't got that low-to-high swing—beginning low at the back and finishing high on the follow through. But it is what happens to the ball on the way which decides the success of the stroke, and your efficiency as a tennis player. You can have the most graceful swing in the world but it is not much use if the ball is always finding the net or the fence. Although it is nice to look stylish on court, it is even nicer to win points.

Think about the strike zone

My advice is not to be preoccupied by things like taking the racket back, getting your feet into the correct position and so on. Worry about that point of contact, the vital moment when the ball actually meets the racket. The ball should be in front of you and no matter where your head is or your feet are, that is where your racket face should be, too.

Think about that strike zone and I've got news for you: you won't have to remind yourself to take the racket back. You will find yourself doing it automatically. If the ball is coming at you fast, the racket will go back fast as you focus your mind on the job of getting the strings of your racket to the ball. As soon as you know the direction of your opponent's stroke, start moving, think about making contact and let the rest come naturally.

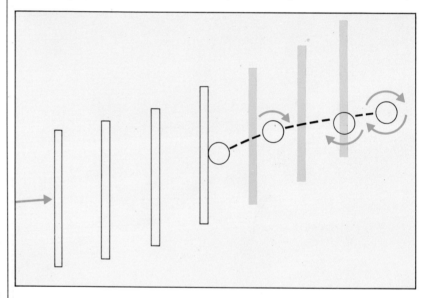

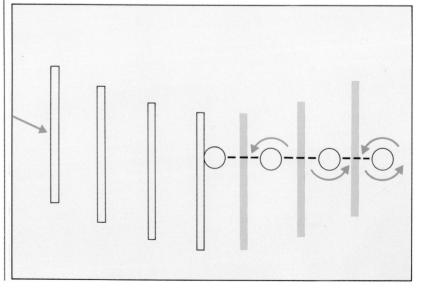

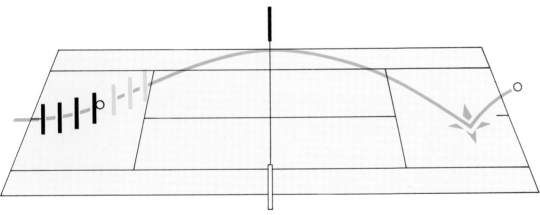

There is no such thing as a completely 'flat' stroke. In making a tennis shot you rarely impart no spin at all to the ball. The spin might be slight but it is there, even with Jimmy Connors who hits the ball as flat as anyone in top tennis. It is the swing which generates spin on the ball not the angle of the face of the racket. In both topspin and slice the racket face should be vertical on impact with the ball. Leave it to the swing to add the spin: topspin from low to high; slice from high to low.

Topspin strokes (above left) have more depth and safety and keep your opponent at the back of the court if they are played well. You can hit the ball as hard as you want and it will still fall deep into court. Tennis is a lifting game anyway and applying topspin is a natural progression from bringing the racket up from low to high.

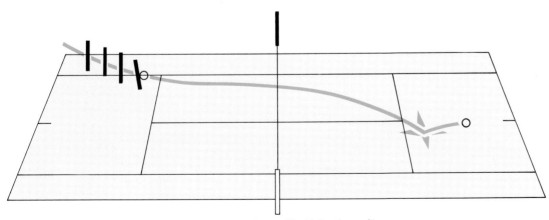

Slice or underspin (above and left) is more defensive. It is also the basic shot for an approach forehand or backhand. Slice keeps the ball low if you are going to the net, forcing your opponent to hit up as the ball dies. It demands precise timing. The high to low action means you have a smaller area of contact with the ball and less margin for adjustment.

Mastering the forehand

Just because the forehand is the shot which is taught first by coaches does not mean it is the easiest. Billie Jean discusses grip, swing and stance and advocates the use of topspin.

If you will forgive the anatomical contradiction, I want to get something off my chest about the forehand. I was in my late twenties before I realized what was wrong with my forehand, and I would like to help you avoid the trap which was set for me when I was a young girl, learning how to play the game.

Back in 1955 I was taught to hit the forehand with an outstretched arm, the idea being that this aided the freedom of the swing and encouraged the feeling that the racket was an extension of the arm. I believe that there are too many limitations to that theory. It is, in my opinion, incorrect and inadvisable.

The backswing

I would recommend that during the backswing the elbow is kept close to the side. The backswing becomes shorter than if your arm was kept straight, and you get the racket back faster. The bent elbow also allows you to make adjustments depending on how close the ball is to your body. You have a little slack to work with. With a straight arm most of your adjustments are with the wrist, which calls for split-second timing.

After you have hit the ball, you uncoil, straightening the arm and finishing up with the high follow through which is essential to complete the shot. If you are having forehand problems, try what I did and keep the elbow in. My only regret is that I did not try it earlier, even if it does go against an established tenet of the game.

All right, some top players like Bjorn Borg and Sue Barker are exceptions to this rule in that they bring the racket across the body and do not follow through in the traditional sense. But generally speaking it is a good habit to bring the racket through in the direction that the ball is travelling.

Hitting the ball

Let us start from the ready position. The feet should be spread apart about the width of your shoulders, your knees should be slightly bent, and you should be focusing on the ball. Always take the racket back early, keeping the wrist firm and the elbow in.

Pivot to the right, then come through—low to high—hitting the ball at about waist height and making sure that you keep the racket roughly parallel with the ground at the point of contact.

It is usual to shift your weight to the front foot as you strike the ball, but that is not always possible if you are moving or in a position where the last thing on your mind is switching weight from one foot to the other. The alternative is to hit off the back foot with an open stance, as so many European clay-court players do. The important thing to keep in mind all the time is the turn of the shoulders, no matter where the feet are.

A smooth follow through is essential to the completion of the shot. Apart from bringing the stroke to a rhythmic conclusion, the upward movement of the racket brushes topspin on to the ball.

The forehand is not the easiest stroke in tennis, but it is usually the first taught. Out of preference hit the ball with topspin and allow for a good follow through with the racket.

Choosing the best grip

The grip I use for the forehand is the Eastern. This is more generally known as the 'Shake hands' grip because you are virtually shaking hands with the racket handle. If you have trouble discovering the grip, the way to find it is by resting the palm of your hand on the strings of the racket and then sliding your hand down the shaft until you reach the handle. Then tighten your fingers. You're there.

The easiest ground stroke?

I think it is a misconception to regard the forehand as the easiest of the ground strokes. Because it is taught first by coaches it is usually the first tennis shot attempted by aspiring players. But a lot of people—myself included—find the backhand a more natural stroke to produce.

The trouble is that too much emphasis on the forehand at an early age can lead to a neglect of the backhand which becomes a handicap—indeed, almost a phobia—later on. It is so easy to develop a sense of inferiority about your backhand because you have spent twice as much time working on your forehand, and come to regard it as your most dependable shot. That is the reason why there are so many defensive backhands at club level.

Forehand with topspin

Topspin is one of three ways of hitting a forehand drive, and it is the one I prefer. The other ways are slice, with underspin, and flat, with no spin at all. In a topspin shot, the racket rises from knee to waist to shoulder and as a result the ball is drawn into court by its own spin after looping over the net.

The ball might soar high over the net but it will pitch in court. A ball hit with topspin can clear the net by about 8 ft (2.6 m) and still home in on target, about 5 ft (1.6 m) from the baseline. If you used the same force with a sliced or flat forehand, the ball would keep going until it hit the fence. A chipped or sidespin forehand is often the best way of preparing your approach to the net, but to keep rallies going from the back of the court, use topspin.

Perhaps your topspin will not be as exaggerated or extraordinary as that employed by Bjorn Borg. But you can introduce a modified form of topspin to gain depth and consistency in addition to that control of the ball which everybody strives for in tennis.

Practising your forehand

The only way to improve your forehand is by hitting a lot of balls. Practise, practise, practise—in front of a mirror occasionally

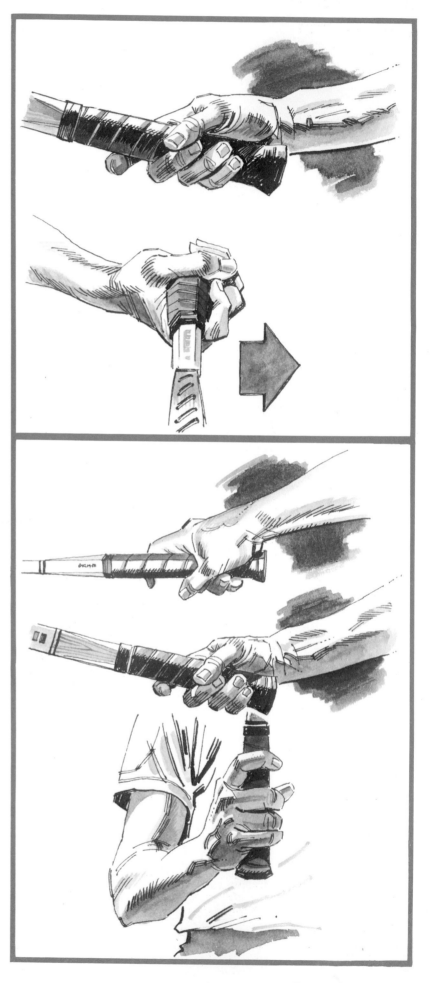

Forehand grips

Left top upper
Continental: To obtain the Continental grip twist the hand about an eighth of a turn to the left from the Eastern. It makes more demands on the wrist, which is why I prefer the Eastern. The Continental is a good grip to use for serving, though.

Left top lower
Western: Also known as the 'Frying Pan' grip. It is used effectively on surfaces where the ball tends to bounce high, and leading exponents include Harold Solomon, Sue Barker and Marita Redondo. Lay the racket down, pick it up and you have the Western grip.

Left below
Eastern: This is the 'shake hands' grip which I use. The way to reach it is to put your hand on the strings of the racket, slide it down the shaft until you reach the handle, and there you are. In my opinion it is the best grip for the forehand.

Body Position and Point of Contact

Below and previous page Take the racket back in a relaxed loop. Then a nice, easy follow through, low to high, keeping the racket head up. Sometimes I drop the racket head too much, but don't fall into the same trap as me! Keep a firm wrist. You should be sideways on, and the shoulders should turn, especially the non-racket arm. The point of contact should be opposite the front foot, and the racket face should be vertical when it strikes the ball.

Halfway stage (left) in the low-to-high movement which goes into the production of an effective forehand drive. The ball will be hit at about waist height with the racket roughly parallel with the ground at that all important moment of impact.

Breakdown of a topspin forehand

Here is another look at the topspin forehand, illustrating that it is the swing which makes the spin. The racket face should be vertical at the moment of impact. This might not seem evident from the shots of Borg and Connors but freeze that split second when ball meets racket and you will see it is true.

if you want to see how your swing looks. You can even practise mentally when you are at the office or relaxing at home. Think about hitting great forehands, and you will end up doing it. As you will have gathered, I am a staunch believer in filling the mind with constructive thoughts!

If things begin to go wrong—and it's amazing how easy it is to 'lose' a shot for no apparent reason—run through the factors that might be the root of the trouble, such as point of contact, preparing too late (start moving as soon as the ball leaves your opponent's racket), allowing the eye to wander, or merely being too lazy to get into position. Tick the possible flaws off mentally like going through a shopping list. It might sound a tall order, but the blemish will be there somewhere.

It is unwise to allow apprehension to tempt you into steering the ball over the net. If you are having trouble with your forehand try to hit your way out of it with strokes born of freedom not anxiety. So you lose: so what? You can't expect to win every match. The bonus is that by hitting the shot as it is meant to be hit, your accuracy and confidence will return. Steering the ball will only encourage more doubt and frustration and eventually a resistance to playing a positive forehand.

What to do with your forehand once you have mastered it might seem obvious—hit the ball over the net, for goodness sake!—but on the other hand it is worth discussing what to do on return of service in singles. On paper, of course, the simplest and most effective way to deal with a serve to your forehand is to whack it back down the line, way out of reach of the incoming server. It is indisputable that this shot is often a winner, but it is just as true that it is extremely hard to produce consistently, so small is the margin for error.

A safer bet is the crosscourt forehand hit with topspin so that it dips to the server's feet. If the angle or height are imperfect you are making your opponent's volley easier, but at least you have a better chance of getting the ball into court than going down

This is the direct opposite to the production of a topspin forehand. High to low instead of low to high. It is a more difficult shot because there is less margin for error. The ball must be met at precisely the right moment or it will end in the net or out of court. Bend the knees and stay down longer to reduce the possibility of error. Use the sliced forehand as an approach shot, to change the rhythm of a rally or if you want to keep the ball low with backspin.

Sliced forehand

the line. Sometimes a low, powerful drive straight at the advancing server can produce a flustered return which gives you the initiative on the next shot.

When you are involved in a lengthy rally use your forehand to switch your point of attack by going both crosscourt and down the line. Once you establish command here it is a fascinating exercise making your opponent guess which way your next forehand is heading. There can be as much bluff and counter bluff in a tennis match as in any spy novel by John Le Carré. Make this the shot that came out of the cold!

It goes without saying that the wrist flicks and body feints which help to disguise the direction the ball is going to take involve a certain amount of risk. Generally speaking, it is more advisable to make up your mind early and do it. But every now and then it is exciting to live dangerously, change your mind and make that late switch which leaves your opponent on the wrong foot. Maybe you are on the wrong foot as well, but hopefully you have won the point.

Points to remember

1 Elbow in during backswing

2 Uncoil arm on follow through

3 Hit low to high

4 Don't allow racket to roll over after contact

5 Keep wrist firm and eye on ball

Make a friend of the backhand

Although most club players treat it with caution the backhand need not be a weakness. It is no harder to produce than the forehand and is a more natural shot if your preparation is right. How to iron out common errors in execution and develop a reliable backhand using one hand or two.

Most club players have problems with their backhand. It is a nagging disability which returns every time they set foot on court. I know some people feel like doing a lap of honour when they actually hit a firm backhand winner. It's like the realization of an impossible dream.

This accounts for so many defensive backhands in the game today. Apprehensive players start their swing high and finish it low as they slice or block the ball back instead of hitting it with a free, upward movement of the racket. It is all part of a malaise born of lack of confidence. Alarm bells start to ring in the mind the moment an opponent drives to the backhand—and, let's face it, this is an almost automatic tactic based on the assumption that the backhand is bound to be weaker than the forehand.

Don't neglect the backhand
As I said in the previous chapter on the forehand, the reason for this imbalance is that newcomers to tennis are invariably taught the forehand first and initially spend most of their time perfecting their timing on that side. But the backhand drive is no harder to hit than the forehand. The belief that it is more difficult is a myth which somehow takes root in the minds of players and grows until it assumes the appearance of truth.

One or two fundamental points can be made about the backhand. First, it is a more natural shot than the forehand because your body is not in the way when you hit it.

Second, it is not difficult to master and once it is mastered you can savour one of the delights of the game: a crosscourt backhand drive, humming with topspin, which dips over the net to the feet of your opponent and makes the ball extremely difficult to return. The inability to make that shot deprives you of a supreme tennis pleasure.

Tennis has had some great backhands: Don Budge, Ken Rosewall, Rod Laver, and Arthur Ashe; Bjorn Borg, Jimmy Connors, Chris Evert-Lloyd, and Tracy Austin with their two-handers. A lot of top players, myself included, will tell you that they consider the backhand to be their best shot—or at least the one they enjoy playing most. Believe me, it is worth doing everything you can to make a friend of your backhand.

Avoid the common faults
The backhand is essentially a smooth, graceful and simple shot. Do not approach the ball with arms flailing like a crazy windmill. Take it nice and easy. Make that swing flow as you sweep away all the worries you ever had about making a stroke that really glides when it is hit properly.

Common faults among backhand sufferers are hitting the ball too late, and not turning the shoulders. But let us go through the shot from the beginning. First, the grip. To find the backhand grip, turn the hand an eighth to a quarter further behind the handle from the Eastern grip I recommended for the forehand. If you want to put your thumb up the back of the handle

I love playing anything on the backhand side—ground strokes or volleys. It is a shot which came naturally to me from the start. I don't have to think—I just do it. Slice, topspin, sidespin—I can hit them all with equal confidence, and satisfaction.

for added reinforcement, that's fine.

Adopt a relaxed, ready position. Be alert by all means, but try not to tense up because you are protecting what you mistakenly believe is your weaker side. There is no earthly reason why your backhand flank should be more vulnerable than your forehand.

Getting ready

Focus on the ball as it comes towards you, and get into the best place to return it. That means nimble footwork, but this should become routine with practice. Change to your backhand grip as you turn sideways and start moving to the left. Cradle the throat of your racket in your left hand as you watch the ball over your right shoulder.

It is not a bad tip to let your chin touch your right shoulder as you pivot from the waist on the backswing. When taking the racket back, keep the elbow close to the body. Brush the hip with your thumb at the bottom of the swing. Then come up, low to high, keeping the wrist firm all the time.

Hitting the ball

Again, the point of contact with the ball is absolutely crucial. It should be about a shoulder's width in front of you as your right leg crosses your left. Your right shoulder should be sideways to the net. Always hit the ball in front because there is no way you can produce a good backhand from any other position. Once the ball is level with you or behind you, you are on the defensive and in deep trouble.

Topspin or underspin?

The backhand I have described is a topspin backhand. It could be argued that the sliced backhand—using underspin created by bringing the racket down on the ball—is safer. It is certainly used more. Rosewall, who hits one of the greatest backhands ever, uses slight underspin in his shots. But by and large I use and advocate the topspin backhand, not merely because I prefer offence to defence but because I think it is a more positive stroke.

Many club players are conservative in their attitude to topspin; or maybe cautious is a better word. You get the gorilla grippers, of course, who seem intent on going for broke all the time. If they were baseball players they would not be satisfied with anything but home runs and if they were brandishing a cricket bat they would be trying to thump sixes off every ball.

But 90 per cent of people are the opposite. Although they have so much room to work in on the other side of a tennis court, they are afraid of lifting the ball well clear of the net and letting topspin bring the ball

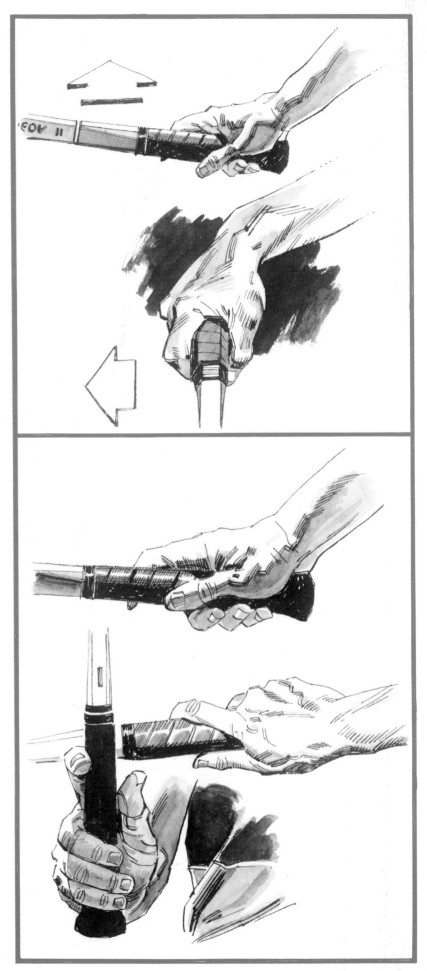

Backhand grip

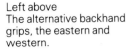

Left above
The alternative backhand grips, the eastern and western.

Left below
To find my backhand grip turn the hand an eighth to a quarter further behind the handle from the Eastern grip I recommended for the forehand. Whether you put the thumb up the shaft of the racket or not is a matter of personal choice. The thumb up the back of the handle makes the grip a little firmer. I vary it. I use the thumb up the back for topspin and high backhand volleys. I tend not to do so on my sliced backhands. It is a matter of what feels best for you.

Backhand preparation

Early preparation is a vital aspect of hitting a reliable backhand. Be relaxed, but be ready too – in good time. Take the racket back as you lock your eyes on the approaching ball, and turn your right shoulder as you pivot. Cradle the throat of the racket in your left hand and brush the hip with the thumb of your racket hand at the bottom of the swing. All this helps towards the sweep and flow of a natural shot which has an undeserved reputation for being difficult.

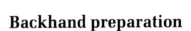

Prepare early. Take the
racket back, turn the
shoulders and focus your
eyes on the ball. Keep the
elbow close to the body,
and brush the hip with
your thumb at the end of
the backswing.

Topspin backhand

Now the follow through. Come up low to high, keeping the wrist firm. Once again the point of contact is crucial to the success of the stroke. It should be about a shoulder's width in front of you, and the racket should be coming up, low to high. If the ball is level with your body, or behind it you are on the defensive and have problems.

down. Top players hate hitting the net. If they are going to make a mistake, they prefer to hit long, not find the net. Never be afraid of giving the ball some air.

To backtrack on the backhand, I cannot over-emphasize the necessity to prepare early. Getting into position and taking the racket back so that you have time to make an unhurried stroke are both essential points if you want to plug a loophole in your game.

The two-handed backhand
Recent years have seen the advent of a whole galaxy of two-handed backhands. Some people use two hands because they have seen the shot employed so well by such remarkable competitors as Bjorn Borg, Jimmy Connors, Chris Evert-Lloyd, and Tracy Austin. At one time coaches at club level tried to discourage the average player from the style but I believe that if the two-hander feels right, use it.

Sliced backhand

For the sliced backhand come high to low, stay over the ball and hit through. Try to keep the racket face vertical at the point of contact. If you open the face too much you will loft the ball out of court. Good timing is imperative.

The Flat Backhand

The Two Handed Backhand

The big virtue of the two handed backhand is that using two hands makes it such a firm and positive shot. It is easier hitting from low to high when you use two hands. It is also a torso shot because you twist your body more in using both hands on the racket. The back shoulder comes round and through. Drawbacks include limitations in reach, and the need for a little more time to get into position. Two handed players experience more trouble in making chip shots. There is no lazy way to play a two-handed drive. You must turn more to get your body behind the stroke, and this leads to solidity of shot. If it feels comfortable, use it.

Usually the racket is held with both hands in the Eastern grip, with the right hand closer to the heel of the racket if you are a right-hander (the opposite applies, of course, for left-handers). The main draw-back of the double-hander is that you need a little more time to play the shot. There are problems of reach and footwork which you don't get when you use one hand, and the style can be cumbersome when you are hitting balls which bounce other than at waist height.

Most two-handers go low to high naturally so they find it easier to generate topspin. And although it involves more rotation of the torso it can be a steadier, stronger shot than the one-handed back-hand.

Players with two-handed backhands often started hitting the ball like that when they were children, and needed two hands to hold the racket. The style becomes in-grained and if the player feels comfortable there is no need to change it. The decisive factor is whether the ball is going over the net with confidence and authority, which-ever style you choose.

A weak backhand helps you lose
You have to settle for the fact that your backhand is going to be a target in most of the matches you play. Such is the shot's reputation for being difficult and a tra-ditional source of weakness that it has become *the* place to attack. You probably don't need me to tell you that, because I'm sure you do it yourself!

Let us imagine that you are receiving service at 15—30, 15—40 or 0—40 down. Where is the service ball going to come, nine times out of ten? Right! On your backhand—and it really is imperative that you acquire the confidence and skill to get the ball back over the net if only to earn the privilege of making another shot. The abs-ence of a reliable backhand gives your opponent a licence to win points.

Volleyers quickly learn to pummel weak backhands without mercy, because it is the quickest way to end a rally. At the same time, another torture to be endured by backhand cripples is the soft, high ball which forces the recipient to seek the pace he or she finds it impossible to generate.

All these warnings are merely to under-line the importance of a dependable back-hand. Keep trying and one day the stance, the footwork and the swing will all fall into place like the pieces of a jigsaw, and you will be up there with Budge, Rosewall, Laver and Ashe. Well, maybe not as far up the ladder of fame as that—but at least the possessor of a deeply satisfying shot that was once a major obstacle to your tennis progress and enjoyment.

Points to remember

1 Hit ball a shoulder's width in front of you

2 Touch thumb on left hip during backswing

3 Prepare early by turning shoulder

4 Hit low to high

5 Keep wrist firm

Serving to win

How to handle the most vital shot in tennis from toss to backswing to point of contact and follow through. The different types of serve. The importance of having a reliable second delivery. Accuracy and depth are more important than uncontrolled speed.

Although the service was first introduced merely as a means of getting the ball into play, it has become the most important stroke in the modern game.

It starts and sets the tone of rallies. If it is working well it gives an enormous psychological lift to the rest of your game. It is the only shot over which a player has complete, uncluttered control from the toss to the moment of impact.

So why are there so many poor serves around? The service court, measuring 21 ft (7 m) long by 13 ft 6 in (4.5 m) wide, is by no means a tiny target. Yet from the baseline it often seems the size of a matchbox to the server anxious to avoid the net and start a rally in a purposeful way.

Apprehension often leads to a breakdown in co-ordination. A feeble serve is usually a sporting instance of the left hand not knowing what the right hand is doing.

A mental approach
Don't think of TOSSING the ball up. Think of PLACING it. You are in complete charge of where you want the ball to go. So PLACE it. Meanwhile your racket arm should be getting ready for that throwing action which is the basis of every good serve. But take it slowly and rhythmically. Don't rush or allow yourself to be rushed.

So many club players strike the wrong tempo with their service action. A quick toss is followed by a hurried backswing and then everything slows down so that the eventual serve is nothing more than a pat over the net, begging to be slammed back

for a winner. It should be just the opposite.

Take your time, place the ball precisely where you want it to be, take the racket back slowly and then attack the ball. To dip into the language of ballroom dancing, it should be slow, slow, quick, not quick, quick, slow, if you want to make the receiver feel like a wallflower.

Practise throwing the ball
In serving you throw the racket head at the ball and this often presents problems for girls, who do not find the action easy. Most girls are not taught to throw the ball properly, hence the phrase 'You throw the ball like a girl'. This can obviously lead to snags with service so I recommend that for practice purposes girls should go out and throw a ball against a wall or a fence. Just get used to that feeling of taking the arm over your head and throwing. It will work wonders for your service, strengthen the arm and silence those taunts.

The serving position
The stance must be as relaxed as the mind is clear. In singles stand just to the side of the centre line. If you stray too far from that midcourt position you leave gaps which invite winning returns down the line. In doubles, where court and net coverage is shared with your partner, the serving position is nearer the sidelines.

To safeguard against the possibility of foot faulting, stand a couple of inches behind the baseline, or more if it makes you feel happier. Racket and ball should be

The service is the one tennis stoke over which a player has total charge. The server places the ball where he wishes on the toss, and it is his decision when to hit it and in which direction. It should be a simple enough process, but many players find it hard to strike the right balance of rhythmic co-ordination.

touching as you face the direction in which you intend to serve. The forward foot (left for a right-hander) should be a shoulder's width in front of the back foot. Point your front shoulder towards the target.

The object now should be smooth co-ordination. The service should be one flowing movement, not a collection of disjointed segments. Again, do not be hustled. You are in charge. Build up a mental picture of where you are aiming at and you will increase your chances of finding the spot.

Holding the racket
Most people use the backhand grip. Whether you hold two balls in your free hand or just one is a purely personal decision. If you have two and get your first ball in, you face the prospect of completing the rally carrying the other ball in your hand. If you put the second ball in your pocket there is a slight delay involved in digging it out when you are trying to concentrate on serving. You will have to choose the method which makes you feel most comfortable.

The serve begins with both arms working in unison; the toss should coincide with the start of the backswing. Without this liaison between the arms your whole action will lack discipline and drive so it is worth working on this aspect.

How high to throw?
First—the toss. To find out the height you should throw the ball, take the racket to the top of your service swing and stop when your arm is fully extended. Make a mental note of the position because that is where the ball ought to be when you hit it.

Roscoe Tanner hits the ball at the top of the toss and Cliff Richey actually strikes the ball while it was on the way up. But for most top players the ball has dropped about an inch when they make contact. They try not to think in those terms. Their aim is to strike at the summit of their swing, with the ball at its apex. Nevertheless, it is advisable to throw the ball an inch or two higher than your extended racket can reach.

The backswing
During the toss the right arm is taking the racket down and round in a deep arc until the racket is well behind the body. A snap of the wrist at the point of contact gives the serve its final impetus.

But do not cock the wrist, ready for detonation, until you have taken the racket so far back that it resembles a back scratcher pursuing an elusive source of irritation in the small of your back. You are now coiled with knees bent and back arched, ready to unwind.

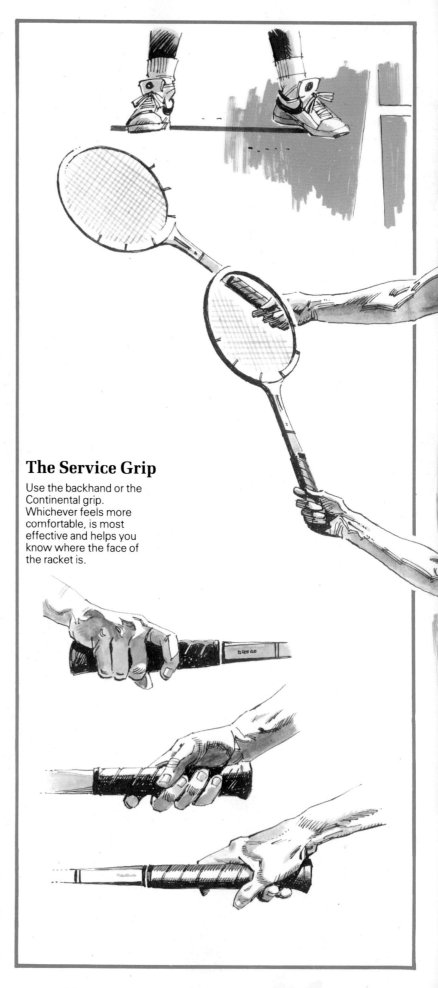

The Service Grip

Use the backhand or the Continental grip. Whichever feels more comfortable, is most effective and helps you know where the face of the racket is.

The Toss

There are two important things to remember about the toss. The first is don't hold the ball too low in the hand, like on the palm. Hold it with the fingers. Also don't forget that you are in charge of where the ball goes. So don't think of tossing the ball up. You are *placing* it where you want it to be. Don't release the ball too soon. Hold on to it as long as you can. Then keep the head up, the chin up and watch the ball as the racket arm comes over with that throwing action which is the basis of every good serve.

Getting it together

Think of the movement of a rocking chair and you have a rough idea of the motion called for in serving. At the time of the toss and the backswing, the weight is transferred to the back foot. Then weight is shifted to the front foot as the racket returns to keep its appointment with the ball.

The elbow is kept high and you are on your toes as the racket comes over for that crucial, body-stretching moment when the wrist snaps the racket forward in the throwing action I described earlier.

The racket follows through, crossing the body from right to left as your back foot swings rhythmically forward, carrying you into court ready for the return. You have completed the stroke which could hold the key to your whole game.

There are several types of serve: the cannonball or flat service, slice and American twist. The cannonball and slice are produced with the same basic action just described but there are variations in toss and swing.

Cannonball or slice

For the flat serve (really there is no such thing because even the flattest of serves has a touch of spin), the toss should be to the right and about 18 ins (50 cm) in front of you. For the slice the ball is placed further to the right.

Slice means sidespin in serving parlance. The racket is taken around the outside of the ball instead of meeting it head on, as in the flat serve. Although the flight might be slower, it is more accurate than the cannonball and its curve from right to left means it has to be received with respect.

Left-handers can have a great time with the slice service. John McEnroe's wicked use of slice makes his serve to the backhand court one of the hardest to receive in tennis. The receiver is taken way out and usually ends up presenting McEnroe with a simple volley into a deserted court.

The American twist

The American twist or kick service is an excellent choice to use as a second serve, but not easy to perfect. My advice is to master the other two serves before moving on to the more advanced demands of the twist.

The ball is placed above the left shoulder and hit with an up-and-over motion. This necessitates more arching of the back and puts added stress on the arm. But without exposing yourself to undue risk of physical strain it can be a useful addition to your repertoire.

The ball must be hit hard, and the up-and-over spin creates a looping trajectory ending in a high kick to the left. The

The Wind up

Try to strike the right tempo with your service action. A lot of club players use a quick toss followed by a hasty backswing and then slow everything down until the eventual serve is just a pallid pat over the net. It should be exactly the opposite. Place the ball precisely with your toss, take the racket back slowly and *then* attack the ball.

Position of feet

The simplest rule about the position of the feet while serving is that they should be in a straight line, with the front foot pointing towards your opponent. As the racket comes forward the back foot should come

Point of contact and follow through

The point of contact for the serve should be as near as possible to the top of the toss. The head should be up, the eyes rivetted on the ball and the body at full stretch.

Hit the ball *forward* not down with a snap of the wrist at the moment of impact. Allow the racket to come through and complete its swing, from right to left.

through too. At the point of contact the back foot should be in line with the front foot. As the racket follows through, crossing the body from right to left, the back foot continues to swing forward.

Back view

This rear view shows how on the backswing the racket is taken to a position where it resembles a back scratcher. Meanwhile the server is coiled with knees bent and back arched, ready to unwind and bring the racket forward to meet the ball.

The serve from start to finish

This sequence of pictures depicts the various stages in the production of the most important stroke in the modern game. Always remember it is the only shot over which a player has total control from the toss to the moment of impact.

There is a lot of truth in the saying that a player only as good as his second service. We all know the tearaway servers whose second ball is a powder puff parody of its predecesso – almost imploring to be slammed back for a winner. The moral is try to hit both your serves with control and depth. Considering the high percentage of thunderbolt first serves that miss the target, dependability plus depth are much more advisable than undisciplined powe Accuracy and consistency will help to banish the spectre of the double fault.

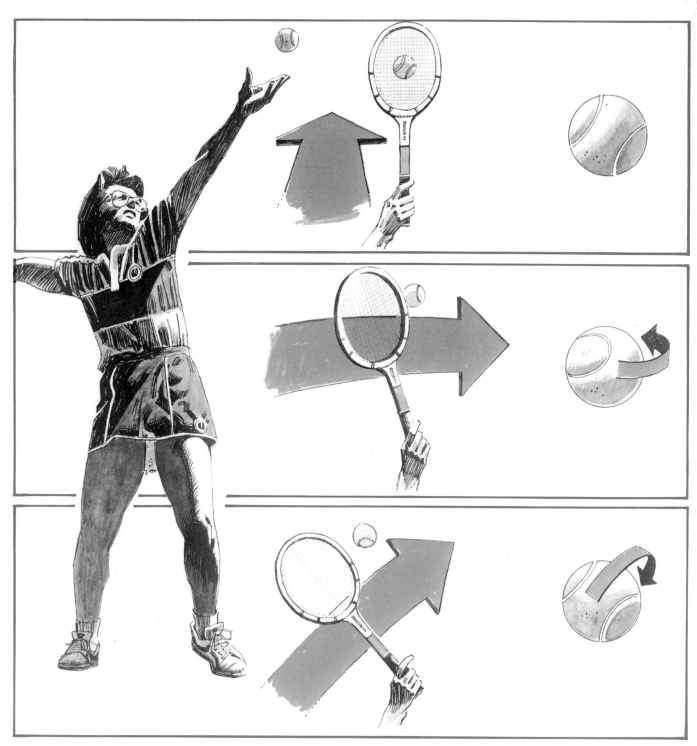

Three types of serve

Flat: Really there is no such thing because even the flattest of serves has a touch of spin. Let us say that the flat serve is hit with the least amount of spin. The toss should be to the right (for the right handed player) and about 18 ins (50 cm) in front of the body.

Slice: In the parlance of serving, slice means sidespin. Although the flight of the ball might be slower, a good slice serve has to be treated with respect as it curves on target from right to left. The ball is placed further to the right and the racket moves across the outside of the ball instead of meeting it head on as in the flat serve. John McEnroe's slice serve is one of the hardest to receive in tennis.

Topspin: The swing is low to high and the racket, moving from left to right, brushes the back of the ball at a 45 degree angle. The toss is more to the left, and behind. The American twist is an exaggeration of this with the ball placed above the left shoulder and struck with an up-and-over motion. It calls for more arching of the back and places added stress on the arm – so be warned!

receiver knows what is on the way but that does not make the serve any easier to take, such is its unpredictable bounce.

The second serve

I suppose that one of the oldest clichés in tennis is that a player is only as good as his second service, but like a lot of hoary old sayings it comes pretty close to the truth.

You might be the fastest server in the world, but you cannot hit the bullseye every time with that thunderbolt first ball. In fact, you will be extremely fortunate if you get two-thirds of your first serves in. Then it all depends on that second serve, the ball which gives so many club players the shakes because failure means a deflating double fault and loss of a point. Better to have a dependable second serve than a swashbuckling but erratic first delivery.

Accuracy and depth are the vital service components for most players. It is marvellous if you are tall and strong and can use those physical assets to power down big serves. But if you are Mr or Ms Average, go for consistency in getting the ball in. Even if you are stuck with a frying pan service action you find it impossible to change, you can still survive by hitting it deep. Think of Frankie Durr, and take heart!

Practising

The service is, of course, one stroke you can work on without anybody on the other side of the net. I know it is a solitary exercise to go out with a couple of dozen balls and just serve. But it does your swing a power of good. Put something in the corners of the service areas—a towel or a ball box—and try to improve your grouping. Patience and industry will pay handsome rewards the next time you are serving for victory, or to stay in a close match.

I have left one critical point to the last. Never hit down on a service ball. When I make contact in serving, inwardly I am saying 'Up and out'. This is my own mental shorthand for hitting *away* from me—getting height on the ball as I drive it deep. Think of hitting the fence, not the net, and you will soon get the hang of what I mean.

All this might seem an awful lot to absorb for the production of one tennis shot but practice and habit can lead to a rhythmic consistency which will not let you down in the tension of a tight contest. It is certainly worth working hard to acquire an effective service which has the twin virtues of improving your morale while damaging that of your opponent, who might start to worry that the loss of his own service could cost him the set. For most players the service acts as a barometer to the state of the rest of their game. In other words, if they are serving well, they are playing well.

Points to remember

1 Slow backswing fast follow through

2 Head up with eyes focused on ball

4 Hit ball forward, *not* down

5 Full stretch at point of contact

3 Shift weight from back to front foot

6 Keep front shoulder up and pointed towards target

The lob in offence and defence

The lob should be in every tennis player's repertoire. It is the great deflator and can be used in attack or defence. When and how to use one of the most valuable, if maligned, shots in the game.

If tennis strokes were human, the lob would be suffering from a massive inferiority complex. In some areas of the game, particularly at club level, it is often regarded with something approaching contempt—the last resort of an indifferent player. Yet this much maligned shot should be a vital part of everyone's tennis armoury.

Watch the professionals. You will not see any of them treating the lob as though it has leprosy. It is frequently the only shot which can possibly haul you out of a tight corner. It can be offensive as well as defensive. Used intelligently, the lob is a source of concern to any opponent whose favourite place is at the net, teeth bared, waiting to pick off volleys.

What the lob can do

Lobs are great deflators. Good lobbers can send their opponents scurrying to the back of the court, draw them up again and then send them back to the baseline in a to-and-fro rally which costs the runner a lot of energy. A lobbing campaign also calls for a vast amount of overhead work in reply, and this, too, can be tiring.

Most of all, though, the lob gives you time to gather your wits and your resources. If you are in a terrible jam—in singles or doubles—a lob earns you the breathing space to restore your defences.

When you are down and almost out in tennis terms, there are few more comforting sights than a lob which you have managed to manufacture from a desperate position sailing out of reach of your rival.

The defensive lob

There are two types of defensive lob and both are as simple as they are effective. One is sliced into the air when you are trapped and have no option but to return the ball by bringing the racket under it and lofting the ball as high as possible. Instinct is usually the best guide here.

The other defensive lob is a more calculated stroke hit from behind the baseline or some other distant part of the court. You hit through the ball in the same way as a ground stroke except that you are driving the ball upwards. Concentrate on smoothness and keep the ball on the strings as long as possible to increase control. Don't be afraid to go for height and depth. Remember the follow through because without it your lob will invariably drop short.

The attacking lob

Attacking lobs are faster and have a lower trajectory. They are hit with slight topspin and once they clear a player's head and land in court they are usually unreturnable as the whirling ball bounds towards the fence. Bjorn Borg and Chris Evert-Lloyd both make deadly use of this shot.

But be warned. A well-struck topspin lob may be hard to return, but it is just as hard to produce. But if you have good topspin ground strokes you should be able to learn to adapt the same spins for lobbing.

When you hit the ball the racket face should be almost vertical and rising fast. Wrist and forearm are then brought into use to create lift and topspin while taking the

There are two types of lob; offensive and defensive. Concentrate on smoothness and try to keep the ball under control.

The Defensive Lob

With the defensive lob you are trying to buy time. Hit it high whether you slice it into the air from a difficult position or make a more calculated stroke from behind the baseline, or some other distant part of the court. It depends on whether you are in a really tough spot, or have a bit more room to work in. Whatever the defensive situation, hoist that ball high. It will give you time to gather your wits and work your way back into the rally. Keep the ball on the strings for as long as possible and remember to follow through.

racket forward and upwards. Once again, a full follow through is essential.

Don't have any qualms about lobbing. If you have been drawn out of position and your opponent is guarding the net don't yield to the temptation to go for a flamboyant winner down the line. You'll almost certainly lose the point. A lob gives you another chance to regain the initiative. You will know it is working when your rival begins to puff, pant and say unflattering things about the most under-rated stroke in the game.

There is no doubt at all that the best lobs are those which are concealed to the last moment. There is nothing to be gained in advertising the fact that you are going to send a ball soaring into the clouds or the rafters. It is much better to disguise your intention by shaping up as though you are going to produce a ground stroke. The trick is to open the face of the racket immediately before impact and leave your rival stranded in the forecourt like a beached whale.

Indoors it is stimulating to hoist a ball into the lights. Outdoors there is the more subtle pleasure of using whatever breeze is blowing to give the shot a swerving and unpredictable trajectory. The art of lobbing is worth acquiring if only to give a stratospheric touch to your game!

But even if the shot had no other virtues, the lob has the priceless advantage of giving variety to your repertoire. The passing shot remains the usual answer to the volleyer but the net marauder can often get into a groove which makes it hard to pass him with a conventional drive. Enter the lob to break up the pattern and cause the volleyer to have doubts about his dominance at the net.

There is no more sensible tennis dictum than when in doubt—lob, providing the lob is good enough. The easiest direction to lob in is diagonally because you have more court to play with, but the majority of top players prefer to lob to their opponent's backhand corner because the high backhand volley is such a difficult shot to execute. And if you can make your lob pitch within a yard of the baseline you can be sure that your retreating opponent is in more trouble than you are as you regain your breath, poise and optimism.

People who dismiss the lob as a negative shot would do well to remember that ostentation has no claims to being a match-winning attribute. Matches are won by the player who gets the ball over the net more often than his opponent, and is ready to curb the desire to wallop a return if a more realistic way of keeping a point alive is to do something less adventurous, like lobbing. The lob is the shot which can enable you to stay in the fight however gloomy the outlook and no matter how precarious your position.

The Attacking Lob

Use the lob as an attacking shot when you have a chance to put yourself on the offensive. The trajectory is lower because the idea is to give the ball just enough height to clear your opponent. Attacking lobs are usually hit with slight topspin so that once they clear a player's head they whirl away towards the fence. Bjorn Borg and Chris Lloyd are two of the best attacking lobbers in the business.

Point to remember
Lobbing corner to corner gives you the maximum amount of court to aim at

Volleying for speed and excitement

There are no half measures if you want to volley. Go in and hunt for the ball, and always look on the volley as a winning stroke. Never retreat unless you are lobbed, but be ready to improvise with the half volley.

One of the earliest and most exciting discoveries I made about tennis was that you didn't have to let the ball bounce before you hit it. As a child, before I knew the meaning of the word volley, I used to find myself at the net. My coach would say, 'Get on back to the baseline, Billie. You have to learn your ground strokes.' But I would reply, 'No, I like it up here. It's more fun.' That childhood impression has stayed with me ever since.

I think that whether or not you are drawn to volleying is all a matter of personality. You are what you are. I have always enjoyed seeking the ball out at the net and revelled in the imagination and quickness involved in volleying. To be a net player you have to be sharp physically and mentally. You must also possess that burning wish to go forward, even if your legs don't always feel like taking you. It's a hunger to end the rally which is never quite satisfied.

Are you a net player?
Should you go in or should you stay back? The answer to that question requires searching self-analysis. What kind of person are you? Do you feel more comfortable at the back of the court rather than charging to the net? Are you prepared to endure the demands on your energy? These are decisions which each individual has to make himself.

It is difficult for certain types of people to actually *want* to go to the net. Bjorn Borg, for example, is not keen on moving in because he has magnificently dependable ground strokes. But he has become a very good volleyer. Once he commits himself to going in he really goes. He gets up there quickly before the ball is on his side of the net, and hits excellent volleys.

Total commitment is imperative. Once you decide to move forward, do not pause for second thoughts. The player who hesitates usually loses the point. That's one time when you have to be a real tennis tiger. And maybe you could get to like it as much as I do!

Even if you are a natural baseliner as opposed to an instinctive net marauder, you are going to have to volley some time. Your opponent is going to draw you in with a drop shot or a short ball, and suddenly you are up there faced with volleying for the point. Never retreat unless it is in pursuit of a lob.

Deciding on a volley
Reluctant volleyer or not, always regard the shot as a winning stroke—a means of bringing the rally to a crisp conclusion. You had better win it by the second volley. Once you get to three volleys you are invariably in big trouble.

The time to advance, apart from behind your serve, is when the ball lands short, in front of your service line. Get to the ball, hit a deep return and carry on running forward. Don't think, 'Oh my God, what am I doing up here?' Be pleased at the fact that you have taken the initiative, and keep up the pressure from the net.

Ideally, you should try to catch the ball at

Pinning everything on the volley calls for physical and mental sharpness and an instinctive hunger to go forward and end the rally at the net. Not everybody is equipped to become a net marauder. Many people are happier patrolling the baseline. But from an early age I have preferred to move in and try to grab the initiative by hitting the ball before it bounces.

Forehand Volley

Make sure you are in the ready position: feet apart, slightly bent knees, the throat of the racket held lightly in your free hand. Feel comfortable, but alert. Grip the racket firmly, and hit the ball in front of you, ideally at the highest point of its trajectory.

The Half Volley

You play the half volley in a no-choice situation. It is a split second decision when you realise that you cannot make the volley and the only way to return the ball is on the bounce, immediately after it has left the ground. Play it with confidence. The ball is going to come off the court, and if your racket is there to meet it early it will go back over the net. Don't try to blast the ball. Use a short back swing, bend your knees and bring the racket up low to high, making sure that the racket head is vertical on impact.

the highest point of its arc. I know that a lot of volleys are hit off the shoe strings from force of circumstance. But always try to hit when the ball is higher. Its the difference between an offensive volley and a defensive volley, and the difference can be dangerous.

One useful rule is to adjust your eyes to the level of the ball. Apart from seeing the ball better, you will automatically bend your knees, which is important. Always bend from the knees not the waist. Your knees are the lifts or elevators of your body, so use them to come up and down.

Going to the net puts a lot of stress on your opponent who is forced to go for a passing shot or throw up a lob. I often call the approach shot to a volley an 'assist'. In basketball someone gives you a great pass and you go in and make the two points. In tennis the two points are represented by the volley, and the approach shot is the means of making it possible. Approach shot— volley: they are part of my drills all the time. They go hand in hand.

Preparing for the shot
I know many players are uncertain about where they should stop and prepare to volley as they go in. I think the simplest method is to stop as soon as you see that the ball is about to hit your opponent's racket. Generally speaking, you don't want to be still running when you hit a volley. Do a little jump if you like but be sure to have both feet on the ground by the time the ball

makes contact with the racket of your rival. You are then ready to move in any direction by the time the ball is crossing over the net—not when it is about to bounce.

You have to maintain a firm grip when volleying. Never stop reminding yourself of that. It is something I tell myself repeatedly. I tend to be loose-wristed so I am always saying 'firm wrist' (just in case you wonder what I'm muttering about on court sometimes).

Think deep

Also, don't be afraid of volleying for depth. An effective volleyer cannot afford to just patsy the ball. You must make the ball move *forward* not down. It's a punch, a push, a nudge—any of those words will do. But never a caress, unless you want your volley to be rammed back, down your

throat. And keep that backswing short. There isn't time for any ornate build up when you are at the net, defying someone to pass you.

Think in terms of opposites when you are volleying. If the ball is hit slowly at you, generate your own momentum. If it is struck hard towards you, then you don't have to do as much because you are capitalizing on your opponent's power. If you are faced with topspin, slice your volley. If it's a sliced return you are volleying, try for a little topspin. Go for opposite spins and rhythms.

The grip to use

The grip for the volley is a matter of personal preference. Some players use the grips they employ for their ground strokes in making forehand and backhand vol-

Backhand Volley

The principles are largely the same as for the forehand volley, and half volley although the point of contact should be a little further in front. If the ball is driven straight at you when you are at the net, take it on the backhand volley.

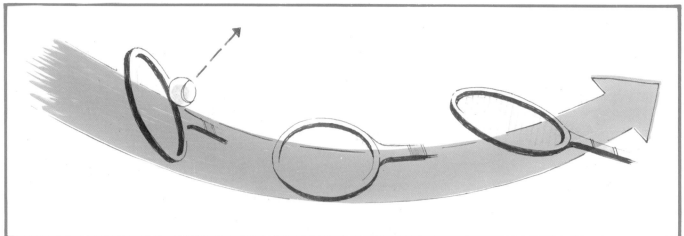

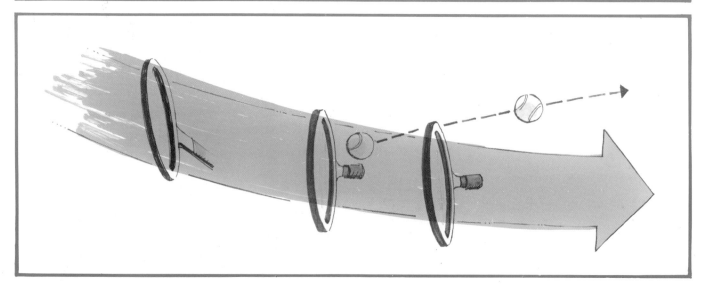

Variations

Here are a few variations on the volley which you might attempt when you are feeling both confident and adventurous. The drop volley follows the same principle as the drop shot in that it 'dies' immediately it clears the net: the lob volley is hit with a tilted racket which lofts the ball back over your opponent's head and the drive volley is a full blooded thwack at a high return.

114

leys—but this means switching grips in mid-rally.

One paramount rule of volleying is to hit the ball when it is in front of you. Don't wait to be introduced. Greet the ball by reaching out for it with the racket, and make sure it has a warm welcome! Fight the temptation to freeze in admiration when you have hit a volley which fills you with pride. While you are standing there thinking what a marvellous shot it was, your opponent is likely to ruin your reverie by returning the ball for a winner.

The ready position

The ready position is the same for both the forehand and the backhand volley: feet apart, slightly bent knees, the throat of the racket held lightly in your free hand. The stance should be comfortable, but inwardly you should be as sensitive as a seismograph—alert to every movement of the ball you are determined to intercept.

Hitting the ball

Try to keep your wrist firm and don't let the racket head sag. Aim for a sideways hitting position—although this is not always possible if the ball is travelling back and forth at speed. If someone drives directly at your middle you will find it easier to take the shot on your backhand. And less painful, too!

As I said at the start, the ideal way to volley is to catch the ball at the top of its rise and to hit it between waist and shoulder height. But often a dipping return will have you groping below the level of your knees. You are not going to put this one away so just go for depth with a sharp jab—not forgetting, of course, to bend those legs.

The half volley

Even the most expert and agile volleyers have their embarrassing moments. No matter how swiftly they get into a volleying position sometimes they cannot reach the ball before it has bounced and have to fall back on the half volley. This is a shot which calls for split-second spontaneity as you try to maintain the momentum of your advance to the net without actually hitting the volley you were seeking.

The crucial factor about the half volley is that you should not be afraid to grovel for it. Bend the knees and really get down so that you catch the ball immediately after it bounces. The racket face should be slightly tilted—not too much or you will end up doing a lob—and a short backswing should produce an adequate reply to a difficult return. It is a useful shot to have around when you find yourself the target for a drive aimed at your feet. Half a volley is better than none at all.

Points to remember

1 Try to hit the ball at the highest point

3 Short backswing then punch forward

2 Hit the ball in front of the body

4 Grip the racket tight and keep the wrist firm

5 If the ball is heading for your middle, take it on the backhand

6 Think deep, not down, unless an easy ball is asking to be put away

The smash: overhead technique

You are not alone if the thought of making a smash brings you out in a cold sweat. But a good player must have confidence overhead. Here are some common sense tips on how to strengthen your game by mastering the most spectacular stroke in tennis.

Answer me truthfully. Are you one of those doubles players who calls 'Yours' and avoids the overhead whenever the opposition lobs. Do you break out in a cold sweat at the prospect of making a smash? Rather than take a smash first time, do you adopt the more cautious method of letting the ball bounce before returning it?

Then read on. And don't worry—you are not alone. You are a member of that great army of club players who tend to make a hash of their smash. Maybe it's that long wait for the ball to fall within reach. Maybe it's the feeling that all eyes are on you as you prepare to make contact. Whatever it is, thousands of people rarely taste the thrill of making the most spectacular shot in tennis. Even when they do produce a successful overhead, the satisfaction is overshadowed by a feeling of relief.

Most top players have good overheads. If they didn't they would just have to dump their rackets and forget tennis. On the circuit you must have a reliable smash or you would be lobbed to distraction and defeat every time you went on court.

The smash is a difficult shot, but it need not be so hard that it paralyses your confidence. One thing is beyond argument: without a reasonably sound overhead you have a serious weakness which will throw your whole game out of balance until it is corrected.

Keep the ball in front

I think that the most common error in making the smash is letting the ball fall behind the body. You must keep the ball in front of you, otherwise you can't see it. You don't have eyes in the back of your head, so keep your sights on the ball.

All of this emphasizes the importance of correct positioning. As soon as you see the ball leave your opponent's racket and realize that a lob is on the way you must start moving into the right place to return it. Turn sideways and take the racket back. Raise your free hand in the air and, if it helps, point to the ball. Keep your chin up and watch the ball as though you are under hypnosis.

The first two steps on an overhead should be quite big—quick, but big enough to reach a position roughly under where the ball is going to descend. Then you take smaller steps to adjust your stance, bearing in mind that the ball should never be allowed to fall behind you.

A morale-raising drill for shaky smashers is to have someone hit you a lob and, without your racket, run back, stand and catch the ball with your hands in front of your body. Do it over and over again until you have the feeling of keeping the ball in front of you. It is so important, and the drill will help to implant the message in your mind.

Getting the shot right

The action for an overhead is like that for a serve except that you use an abbreviated backswing. It varies from person to person but for the average club player I would recommend cutting out the full, down-and-

The smash is the most spectacular shot in tennis. It could never be described as easy but once mastered there is little in tennis terms to equal the thrill of hitting a descending ball back into your opponent's court. The lack of a reasonably sound overhead is a serious weakness in anybody's game.

Letting the lob bounce

You should try to hit an overhead before the ball has bounced but some lobs are too high and well judged to be smashed while they are in the air. If you have no choice but to let the ball bounce, watch it closely, take care with your positioning and make your smash at the highest point of the ball's bounce.

round swing. Instead, take the racket up immediately until it is behind your back, cocked for action. The simpler the movement the better.

Point your front shoulder where you want the shot to go. Then strike the ball as if you were hitting a flat serve with a throwing motion of the racket head, and the arm at full stretch. Above all, resist the urge to peep at where the ball is intended to go before it has got there. This is one of the reasons why so many smashes go awry.

Just as many golfers fail to keep their head down, tennis players are prone to anticipate where their smash is heading by moving their gaze from ball to target. Don't do it. Keep your head up until contact has been made and the ball is well on its way. That is the time when you can allow yourself the luxury of observing what damage you have done to the opposition.

If the ball bounces
Some lobs are too high and well judged to be smashed while they are in the air—although you should always make that your aim. If you have no choice but to let the lob bounce, watch the ball closely, position yourself carefully and make your smash at the highest point of the bounce.

So many players rarely experience the thrill of making a good smash. They wait for the ball to fall within reach and the fear of being made to look an idiot if they miss it inspires trembling apprehension. Following simple rules can take much of the difficulty out of the stroke as these photographs show.

The Action

The action is like that for a serve except that you take an abbreviated backswing. Take the racket back immediately and point your front shoulder where you want the ball to go. Hit the ball as if you are hitting a flat serve with a throwing motion of the racket head and the arm at full stretch. You can get more angle if you are close to the net. Otherwise go for depth.

Position for the smash

Always keep the ball in front of you and well in sight. Turn sideways and take the racket back, raising your free hand in the air and pointing to the ball. The first two steps should be quite big but take smaller steps to adjust your stance. Keep the head up and watch the ball not its intended destination.

Always be firm and decisive. An apprehensive attitude will be reflected in a nervous shot. And—to return to something I have stressed in previous chapters—don't be obsessed with hitting the ball *down* unless it is an absolute set-up two feet from the net. Think of *depth*, and using the full length and breadth of the court. As long as your point of contact is all right, the ball will go in.

Get into the habit of hitting the ball forward, not down. If you are not already doing this the place to start is the practice court. Develop your confidence there and you will soon be shouting 'Mine', not 'Yours', when your doubles opponents start bombarding you with the lobs that can tease, torment and tantalize unless they receive the strongest of replies.

It is nice to hit a smash into which you have poured every ounce of your weight and energy. Nice, but not always necessary. The baleful, bionic smash delivered with subconscious flames pouring from the nostrils can sometimes mean that the player has allowed force to overshadow accuracy. And the hardest smash in the history of tennis is worth nothing at all if it lands in the net or pitches out of court. So it makes sense to put intelligent placement before naked power.

If you can already hit a straightforward smash with a degree of confidence it is a good idea to give some thought, and practice, to angling your overhead. A firm smash deep to either corner of the court is a pretty good shot in singles because the speed of the ball will usually be too much for your opponent to handle and he won't be able to return it.

But the angled smash is an excellent stroke in doubles. Although it involves split second timing, a twist of the wrist can send the ball in an unexpected direction and confuse the opposition. Beware of using it too often but it is worth cultivating if only to introduce more control into your overhead work. It gives you a pleasing sense of power to know that you can send the ball in several directions, not just the predictable one your rivals are anticipating. The closer you are to the net the more options you have in terms of angle. You can also hit the ball harder, but beware of the high bounce which can give your opponent plenty of time to run it down and make a return.

A dependable overhead has a beneficial effect on your volleying game because it removes that fear of being lobbed when you advance to the net. The moral is don't let the smash become the skeleton in your tennis cupboard. Give the shot flesh and blood, and you will start to feel as unstoppable as the Incredible Hulk!

Points to remember

1 Keep the ball in front and in sight

2 Turn sideways at the same time as you take your racket up

3 Take two side steps to get into position, smaller steps to adjust

4 Keep your head up until after contact

5 Point your front shoulder towards target

6 Think deep, not down

Off court

**Fitness • Exercise • Practice
Health • Diet**

Practice: is it worth the effort?

Tennis demands practice, practice and more practice if you want to improve. It need not be boring if you ring the changes in your practice routines and the benefits in live competition are enormous. Matches are won by shots sharpened on the practice court. Although tennis helps to keep you in shape you will improve your game if you add simple exercises to your daily routine. They need not take long and they will not only ease the creaks and groans but increase your enjoyment and efficiency on court.

Practice might not always make perfect, but the nearest you will ever get to perfection in tennis will be via the practice court. That is where you sharpen the shots which you will later use instinctively in a match.

Live competition is not the time for experiments designed to improve your game. That is what practice is all about: filling your subconscious with thoughts and reactions which become automatic at moments when you don't have time to think about anything else but the point you are playing.

Practice is part of my daily ritual, an integral aspect of my lifestyle. I would feel lost without it, and I make sure that I use every minute in a constructive way. Practice becomes meaningless if it is devoted to repetitive routines with no end product in mind. You might as well have stayed at home.

Strengthen your shots
Be methodical in trying to improve weaknesses. The variations are limitless. Depending on which shot you want to strengthen, work out a system where you lose two points or even a game if you miss the stroke in question.

Play one service ball instead of two to tighten up your serving accuracy. An excellent way of quickening reflexes on the volley is for two, three or four players to stand at the net and fire volleys at each other. That really makes your reactions smoulder.

Players should take turns in 'feeding' the required sort of balls to each other. If you want to compete, vary the scoring. Use the table tennis system, or play the first to get to 10 points with one player doing all the serving and changing sides every five serves.

Practising in threes
Practising in threes is one of the best ways of improving fitness and speed. Two players stand at the net and volley while the player on the other side tries to return the ball first bounce, and must pursue everything.

When tiredness begins to set in the two volleyers move back to the baseline and the third player takes over at the net where he is expected to volley every return and smash each lob. Players take turns in the solo role—and somebody has been slacking if everyone has not been thoroughly stretched and tested by the end of the session.

These are all devices to keep interest high and drudgery low. The moral is that practice need not be boring.

Don't be lazy just because it is practice. Try to take every ball first bounce, as you would do in a match. Concentrate hard, too, because that is something you can develop in practice. Make sure that the habits you pick up on the practice court are good ones.

Always remember to practise your strengths as well as your weaknesses. Sometimes people become so preoccupied with their deficiencies that they neglect the shots they play well.

The efficiency of a stroke in match play is often born on the practice court. Practice is all about picking up good habits which will come in useful during the heat of competition. You are feeding your subconscious so that your reactions will become instinctive when there is no time to pause and think what to do next.

Tennis is a game for individuals and few games
expose personal characteristics so vividly. Your inner
self is there for all to see as the tennis court becomes
the equivalent of a psychiatrist's couch. I have often
thought that a shrewd selling line for the game would
be 'Discover tennis and find yourself'.

Fitness is worth the effort

One of the great kicks of living is being in good shape. Apart from feeling better you are much more productive and lead a fuller life. I know that when I've been really out of shape—notably after operations—the contrast was both marked and depressing. Physical fitness is life's most glittering prize.

Whether tennis on its own is enough to achieve a high level of fitness is a moot point. So much depends on the skill factor. The greater the skill, the longer the ball is in play and the more the body is tested. That's another reason for improving your game!

But most people do not command the expertise needed to make tennis more than a pleasant, relatively undemanding pursuit. It still rates higher than golf as a means of taxing the limbs, the lungs and the heart. But for the average player it falls short of being the complete form of exercise. Something extra is needed.

Yes, I know you are tempted to skip the next few paragraphs. Persuading people to give up 15 minutes of their day for simple exercise is like asking Fort Knox for a loan. But let me try to coax you, anyway.

It is all a matter of habit. First, there is the initial acceptance that a little physical conditioning is good for you. Then there is the discipline involved in making sure that you start doing it. Gradually that discipline dissolves into a habit—a good habit too.

Most of us are lazy. It's natural, I suppose. As far as exercise is concerned I think the knack is to include it as part of your daily routine—not as something separate from the rest of your schedule. If you have to get up and cook breakfast for the family or take the kids to school, for example, you do it because you know it is necessary and has to be done.

Try to adopt a similar approach to exercise. Don't keep putting it off. Make it one of your goals. Make an appointment with yourself the night before. Then wait for that daily appointment to become automatic. It will happen, and you will not regret it. Just 15 minutes a day can make you a better tennis player and add 10 years to your life. And that's what I call a smart investment!

Actually you can begin while you are still in bed, or at least on top of it, by pulling your knees towards your shoulders about 10 times. This stretches the back muscles and tightens the abdomen and is an excellent way of starting your bedroom routine.

For sit-ups and press-ups you need to be on the floor. Sit-ups involve clasping your hands behind your neck and then leaning forward until your elbows touch your knees. You can vary this by extending your

Practice becomes irrelevant if it is given over to mindless routines with no purpose. Sessions on the practice court are built into my daily ritual and I try to ensure that every moment is used constructively. Work hard, and never forget that your strong shots need practice, too. A total preoccupation with weaknesses can lead to the neglect of the shots you play well.

arms in front of you and touching your toes after rising from the flat position. Press-ups are self-explanatory. Pivoting from the hips is also exactly what it says, either with arms on hips or extended as you swing the head and trunk from side to side.

All these simple movements stretch and strengthen muscles and if you hear cracks, creaks and groans, that's fine. That is the sound of important parts of your body being reminded of what they are there for.

I know that a lot of club players cannot be bothered to do any exercising at all apart from the effort entailed in playing. Their only pre-match preparation is grabbing their gear, throwing it into the car and driving off to the club. I would hate to sound pompous about this, but scorning that bit of bonus exercise is reducing their efficiency in competition. It will be the fitter player who makes fewer errors when stamina becomes an important issue in a longish match.

The exercises I have described are comparatively gentle but nonetheless effective. It is better to do a little every day than reserve your physical activity for one heavy tennis session at the week-end which can leave you so full of aches and pains that you need a crowbar to lever you out of bed the following day. If I've whetted your appetite sufficiently, why not try a few warm-up exercises at the club immediately before you play? You will enjoy your game so much more because you will be looser and less liable to strains.

For those who really want to get to grips with fitness I recommend the stretching exercises plus running, cycling, weight lifting or using expanders. Mind you, I write as an unusually energetic convert. I have so much excess energy that I tend to regard sleep as a wasteful intrusion.

If you wear glasses
A funny thing happened to me in the Daihatsu Challenge tournament at Brighton, England, last November. The crowd thought it was funny anyway—and so did my opponent, Martina Navratilova. My glasses fell off during a match for the first time ever. Even I laughed as I tried to finish the rally without them.

It would not have been quite so amusing if my glasses were dropping off all the time, but the fact is that they don't. It was the unusual nature of the incident that caused the hilarity, on and off court.

Losing your glasses in a match is one of the secret dreads of players who are helpless without them. One thing I have found useful is to have wire frames which curl round the ears and keep my glasses secure no matter how hectic the rally. And, as I say, Brighton was the first time that they

Try to include exercises as part of your daily routine if you want to improve as a tennis player. It takes discipline but gradually that discipline becomes a habit which is well worth acquiring despite the initial cracks, creaks and groans of a protesting body. Pictured here are some of the stretching of the stretching exercises I use to keep in shape. Always remember that 15 minutes exercising a day can add 10 years to your life. From a purely tennis angle it is the fitter player who makes fewer mistakes when stamina becomes a critical issue in a long and closely contested match.

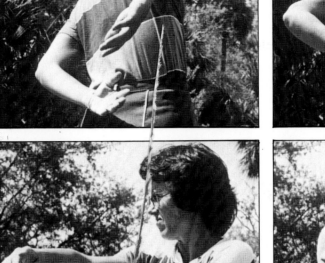

caused me embarrassment by falling off.

I have been wearing glasses since I was 13. I tried contact lenses but could not get the acuteness of vision I needed and returned to glasses. I think that players who wear glasses should definitely get plastic lenses, for safety.

Demisting your glasses

One recurrent problem for bespectacled tennis players is the misting over of their glasses which often happens during a match. They don't have to be reminded of the hold-ups as they wipe their lenses—or the repeated apologies to opponents who sometimes fail to understand the need for the delay.

Here is a demisting method I use when I'm on the road. Take a bar of soap and wash the lens of your glasses. Let them dry a little and then, using a soft paper tissue to avoid scratching the plastic, dry them gently. This leaves a protective film which will help to prevent the condensation that makes you feel as though you are playing in thick fog.

People who wear glasses should not regard them as a handicap on court. At least they make it possible to play. I mean, if glasses hadn't been invented we would be really up the creek, wouldn't we? I can't see two feet without my glasses. With them I have better than 20–20 vision. Need I say more?

More self-explanatory exercises from my daily schedule. They do not take too much out of you. The reason so many club players cannot be bothered to do any exercises is the time involved. But the benefits are so obvious that the really keen competitor must accept that there is more to playing tennis than grabbing your gear, tossing it into the car and driving off to the club. These exercises, like those on the preceding pages are elementary and easy to do. Try them and you will start to play better tennis.

Index

136

Acknowledgments

The publishers wish to thank the following individuals and organizations for their kind permission to reproduce the photographs in this book:
All-Sport:(T. Duffy) 20, 32-33, 33 below, 53, 60-61, (S. Powell) 26-27; Steve Hale: 56-57; Tommy Hindley: 14-15, 16, 17, 19, 65; Leo Mason: endpapers, 37 right; Art Seitz: 18, 24.

Special photography:

Harry Ormesher: 1, 2-3, 4-5, 6-7, 8-9, 10-11, 22, 23, 25, 29, 36-37, 37 above, centre and below, 40-41, 44 above inset, 44-45, 49, 68-69, 68 right inset, 70-71, 73, 76, 109, 117, 120, 121, 124-125, 127, 128-129, 133, 134-135. Martin King: 47, 55, 68 above left inset, 132. Michael Busselle:130-131.

Illustration: George Stokes. Diagrams: Steven Clark

A special thanks to Jacqueline Dineen (editorial) and Dave Allen (design)

Index compiled by Ron Watson